C000070187

'Lancashire Lives'

Book Two
Interviews with and tales of some interesting folk from the Rossendale Valley

including people from
Bacup, Waterfoot, Haslingden, Rawtenstall and Ramsbottom

by Benita Moore A.L.A.

with a foreword by Susan Halstead, Reference Librarian, Rossendale District Libraries

Lancashire Lives (II)
by Benita Moore A.L.A.

Published by Carnegie Publishing Ltd., 18 Maynard Street, Preston PR2 2AL
First published, December 1991
Copyright ©, interviewees and Benita Moore, 1991

Designed and typeset in Caslon Medium by Carnegie Publishing Ltd.
Printed by T. Snape & Co. Ltd., Boltons Court, Preston, Lancashire

ISBN 0-948789-76-X

Contents

The Grand Theatre (later the 'Palace'), Rawtenstall just before its demolition in 1937.

Foreword

by Susan A. Halstead, Rossendale District Reference Librarian

'Friends, Romans, countryman, lend me your ears.'
(Julius Caesar, Act III, Sc. 2)

Little did William Shakespeare know that these words could be so aptly applied to the recording of oral history in Rossendale in 1991. In this hi-tech world of videos and computers, never has the art of listening been more important. Although we are now more aware of the significance of preserving the past to assist us in understanding the present and preparing for a better future, so much history is locked away in the unique memories of individuals. Benita Moore, in her *Lancashire Lives* series, has given us the key to this treasure trove.

Benita has recorded the reminiscences of ordinary people in Rossendale – mothers, textile workers, shopkeepers, farmers – and their memories paint a picture of life in the early twentieth century which already is a foreign country to the generation growing up today; compare 'you would never see a line of washing out on a Sunday' (Maggie Edwards) with all the activities occurring now on the same day.

All these individuals, describing how they worked at market trading or black pudding making and then how they played – 'we used to go on the swings and make ourselves sick' (Maggie Shore) – may not have been significant in the national scene. However, their words, here set down on paper and preserved forever, are invaluable in terms of local history and, after all, a national jigsaw is made up from a myriad of local pieces.

We are honoured to step into the lives of these Rossendalians – sometimes sad, sometimes happy, but always fascinating – and Benita now invites you to be sitting comfortably, then to begin . . .

Susan Halstead B.A., A.L.A.

Acknowledgements

Grateful thanks to the following: Phyllis Taylor; Edna Baron; Anne Armitage; Margaret Barlow and Aline Watson for photography; James Parsons, Printers, Rishton; Jennifer Shilliday; Chris Aspin and John Davies for photographs; *Rossendale Free Press*; *Lancashire Evening Telegraph; Accrington Observer and Times; Hyndburn Citizen;* BBC Radio Lancashire; Lancashire Libraries, Rawtenstall, for the loan of photographs; Mr D. McClaney and staff, Rawtenstall Library.

A very special thank you to Mrs Phyllis Taylor and to Susan Halstead B.A., A.L.A., for all her expertise and time so freely given.

Thanks also to all those interviewees who couldn't be included in this book, but who will be included in later volumes.

Benita Moore

Introduction

Welcome to the second book in my series of *Lancashire Lives*. This time I have been interviewing some people from different parts of the Rossendale Valley, and very interesting it's been, too.

I myself have lived at Rising Bridge on the outskirts of Rossendale for over twenty years, and have always been delighted with its beauty and Lancashire folklore. The people of the Rossendale Valley are a race unto themselves; hard-working, tough, parochial, zealously guarding their heritage and local traditions; yet I have never met with such kindness and humour.

Everywhere I went, people were always anxious to help and advise me, and their hospitality was truly Lancastrian. Please note that all the interviews in the book are the transcribed words of the interviewees, and that they are responsible for their own statements.

There are many villages and areas of Rossendale which I have not yet been able to cover, but I hope to chronicle people from such places as Weir and Water, Crawshawbooth and Constablee etc. at some future date.

I cannot close without thanking my two stalwart friends, Phyllis Taylor and Edna Baron, for their help in transcribing some of the tapes, and also Ada Gibson who helped in other ways. Grateful thanks to you all.

I hope you enjoy reading this book as much as I've enjoyed writing it.

Benita Moore
Rising Bridge
November 1991

Bertha Clare

Top o' th' Bank Farm, Roundhill Lane, Rising Bridge

'I was six years old when I came to live up here, and I went to Stonefold School. We thought it was wonderful up here in the fields when we moved to Top o' th' Bank Farm.

It was coming up to November 5th and mi dad said we could have a bonfire in our field, so we told all our school pals at Stonefold that they were all invited. Of course, we had to go wood gathering first. In those days there wer only gas lamps on the main road. So mi dad always used to light a storm lamp for us, and one day he said:

'I want you to go up to Billy Hardhead's.' (That wasn't his real name, but we never knew him by any other name!)

It seems he'd been cutting some trees down facing the Farmer's Glory, and there were a lot of branches we could have. He used to cut the trees into logs and burn them with the peat he got from the moor. All the children came along – about ten of them. Well it's a fair walk fer children, but mi dad lit this lamp, and off we went. One of the boys said that he'd ask for the wood, so the rest of us stopped in the lane. He knocked on the door and said:

'Please Mr. Hardhead can we have that wood?'

Billy sez: 'I'll Hard heid you b------s if you're nod off!'; so we come running home.

'You haven't been long,' sed mi dad.

'Oh he swore at us,' we sed.

'Whatever for?' dad asked.

The boy said: 'Well I sed –

please Mr. Hardhead can we have the wood?'

'But he's not called Mr. Hardhead – he's called Mr. Grimshaw,' mi dad told us!

Anyway, mi dad sed he would see him because he used to come down to the Rising Bridge Inn at 12.30 everyday. He went to th' end o' th' path to catch 'im and he sez:

'Bill thy are a skinny devil anyway.'

'What for?' sez Bill.

'Well I sent t'children up fer some bonfire wood yisterday,' he sez: 'They'll clear that grass for tha, and tha's getten what tha wants.'

'Well,' sez Bill: 'If they'd come an' asked mi proper it would 'ave bin different.'

'Childer didn't know,' mi dad told 'im: 'You know verry well everybody calls you that.'

'Well alreight – tell 'em to come up, bud I want an apology.'

So when I come 'ome from school he lit lamp fer us and we all trails up again. So Jim Roberts who'd knocked on t'door before knocked again. He said:

'We're very sorry Mr. Hardhead but we didn't know you were called Mr. Grimshaw.'

He sed: 'Well that's alreight then. Clear id all eaut, and when you've done mek sure you shut t'gate.'

Well it come to November 5th and we had a grand big bonfire in the field. We had to wait fer the older children to light it and we'd fireworks galore – you could ged a bag full o' fireworks then fer not much. When the fire was well

alight, mi mother called me and our Susie in. She says:

'I want you to go to Mrs. Howarth's at Rising Bridge.' (She kept the shop then.) We had to get 5lbs of brown sugar to mek some toffee. All the cooking was done on the fire then. (This was before gas and electricity came to Rising Bridge.)

Well, we had a big iron pan with two handles, and mi mother pulled the hob down. [This was a kind of iron grate which lay across the fire and supported the pan.] We kept coming in to test the toffee to see if it wer ready. Mi dad got fed up with us keep runnin' in and out, so he scrubbed and dried the big slop stone [a stone sink] and poured the toffee in to mek it set quickly. We'd oil lamps then, and mi dad says:

'Now I'll carry it in.'

So he pours the toffee into the sink, but unfortunately mi mother had forgotten to put the plug in – so all the toffee ran down the waste pipe. Off we had to go fer another 5lbs of sugar, but this time the toffee was set in roasting tins, as it should be!

Mother promised all the children that she would send them some toffee to school the following day, so all the children and teachers got treacle toffee at Stonefold school. You see, if the teachers got some we were allowed to eat it in school – we knew what to do then.'

Just tell me about your family. How many brothers and sisters had you?

'I had three brothers and two sisters and we've always been a very happy family. Mi mother and dad did everything with us. It didn't matter how many children come up to play with us, they didn't mind as long as they could see where we were. Our Bill (mi brother) put a swing up for us in th' barn, and we used to run home from school just to be first on the swing.'

What about the school at Stonefold?

'Oh I can tell you some things about school. I went to Stonefold as I said and I was in standard one. Our teacher was Miss Rose, and she was very old, she was a real school marm! The headmaster was a Mr. Garside at that time. Miss Rose must have been well-on into her sixties. Teachers retired at seventy in those days, and she was a real Victorian school marm. Her clothes were always the same – long black skirt and a black silk blouse. Her spectacles were always perched on the end of her nose and her high boots buttoned up the side.

Every Friday we had arts and crafts; needlework and such like, boys as well as girls; there was no woodwork then. We had to make a raffia purse each. On one occasion, one boy called Cyril took his work up to the teacher who said it was all right. These purses fastened with a button and loop, but that was a task for the following week. However, there was Cyril sewing a button on, so the teacher showed him how to make the loop. Then someone in the class started to giggle, and all the children joined in. The ring leader, Noel Grimshaw, was called out by the teacher. That's when we discovered where Cyril had got his button from, because as Noel started to walk across the room his pants fell down. The teacher made Cyril sew that button back on Noel's pants, in front of the class.'

When you left school where did you go to work?

'Well, I left school at 14, and there were seven mills in this area, so naturally I had to go into weaving. I went to Stonefold cotton mill. A man called Bill along with his wife

Bertha Clare and her brother, Bill Barrow, in front of her house in Rising Bridge.

had six looms between them, and they learnt me to weave. The mill owner was Rodwell Worsley. I started as a tenter (a learner); mi wage wer five shilling (25p) per week. I wer tenting fer twelve months. You'd to wait fer someone retiring er dying before you got yer own looms. Eventually, I got two narrow looms (30 inches) from which I earned 15 shillings (75p) a week. When I got married I was earning 25 shillings a week, and that was a good wage. We weren't on th' bread line because fer fifteen shillings you could fill yer shopping bag fer a week; a full 'buying in'.

All the cotton mills have gone now, and weavers are looking after many more looms per weaver so of course less weavers are required.

I wer in the Girl Guides, and we had some lovely times, I wer in till I wer about fifteen. When it was near to my sixteenth birthday, I'd been saving up fer a bicycle. There

was a cycling club in Haslingden called 'Haslingden Wheelers'. There were parents with tandems, and if their children could ride bicycles, they could be members as well. Mi brother was a member so I was saving up fer a bike so I could join.

Anyway, on the Saturday, mi mother and dad were going to mi grandma's at Blackburn, so I went with 'em. Mi grandma says:

'It's your birthday today isn't it?'

Mi dad says: 'Yis grandma, and she's moithering over a bicycle.'

Mi grandma pulled a five pound note out of her purse – it were like a sheet o' paper.

'Tek her to King Street,' mi grandma said: 'And ged her a bicycle.'

It wer a Raleigh! How lovely; wi drop handle bars, and a saddle bag on th' back, I thought it wer wonderful!

'How are we going to get it 'ome?' says mi father.

'I know how she'll get it home, she can stop here tonight and her brother can come for her tomorrow. He can bring her 'ome on th' Top road,' said mi grandad. There were no cars then; it wer all horses and carts.

It wer five shillings to join the cycling club fer twelve months. They met every Monday in a room over a shop. They planned where they were going at the weekend, and we also learned how to read road maps, and how to look after yer bikes.

Anyway, they decided to go to Blackpool on the Saturday. It wer a blooming long way! The Wheelers had a kind of Hostel at Freckleton so we stopped there fer cups o' tea and we had our dinner, then on to Blackpool. It wer a boilin' 'ot day so coats came off and went in the saddle bags. Well, wi got to Blackpool and the leader told us to be at the Pleasure Beach at 5 o'clock or we'd be left behind. We were ready to leave at 5 o'clock, and it was a quarter to eleven when we got home.

'Wherever have you been?' asked mother when I got home.

I wer badly sunburned and went to bed covered in camomile lotion [sic]. The following morning what with sunburn and saddle soreness I wer in a weary state, I ached in every muscle. Mi brother brought out a bottle of embrocation with which he was massaging mi legs. When mi mother came in she nearly had a fit! It seems he'd got the wrong bottle – he wer rubbing mi legs wi furniture cream!'

Did you go to Sunday school?

'Yes. Lizzie Rigg was our teacher, and we had our walking day on a Saturday, and then we had a 'field day' on this field up here in front of the farm. There wer races and games, there wer toffee stalls and ice cream, and the band played.'

Did you have Sunday outings?

'No, we didn't. It was too expensive fer one thing fer people to go on trips. Stonefold was only a village and money was scarce. We were lucky to go to the pictures on a Saturday afternoon. We were given threepence, and had to walk to Haslingden, and back. It wer twopence in the pictures and a penny fer sweets.

Haslingden market used to be all along Deardengate and a man made toffee – a kind of rock. We all got a different flavour, and swopped round, and the toffee was measured accurately so we got a proper share. That was the highlight of our week when we wer children.

There wer two picture palaces in Haslingden: the Empire and the Palace. The Empire was where the Bingo Hall is now. Where the Palace was, in Beaconsfield Street, is now a furniture warehouse. When we grew up and went to the pictures, it wer sixpence (2½p) unless you were well off – then you went in the ninepennies; plush seats and all that. I used to take another girl with me to the pictures every Saturday afternoon. There was always a serial, fourteen er fifteen episodes.'

Was your father a farmer?

'Well when we come up here it was a poultry farm. Mi dad was a collier and he made it into a poultry farm.'

Did you have a Maypole on Mayday from the Sunday school?

'No, but we had our own among the children, but that's all gone now.'

Where did you live when you got married?

'We went to live in Hud Hey and we paid seven shillings (35p approximately) a week rent. I was married in 1939; war broke out then. Mi grandmother in Blackburn died in 1941, so mother and dad went to live at Blackburn in the house owned by mi grandmother. None of mi father's family wanted to live at the farm, so mi husband and I came to live here and we've been here ever since. During the war it wer terrible, we were away from any street lights and everything wer blacked-out. There was a gas lamp up to the Farmer's Glory and nothing in between! Of course, all the lamps were put out anyway during black out. We had to have black curtains, and if we used a torch it had to be covered so that no light was visible from above.'

Were you still working in the mill when you came up here?

'Oh yes – Stonefold Mill had closed down so I went a working up Duckworth Clough, then that closed down as well. There were so many men in the forces there weren't enough workers to keep the mills running.

As I said, the street lights were gas lamps, and the gas-lighter was nicknamed 'Owd Flare-up' because the light always flared-up when he pulled the chain which turned the gas on. I can see him now – he always wore a right long jacket, and a cap tied on with a scarf, because he was out early morning in all weathers.'

So though it's still rural round here it was even more so in those days?

'Yes.'

What about Carter Place Hall, that building was there then wasn't it?

'Oh yes. They were cotton manufacturers that lived there – one of the Worsleys who owned the mills in this area. They had servants and horses and carriages. Oh yes; proper gentry they were! I could tell you a lot more Benita, but maybe you've heard enough.'

Bertha is still at the farm, which has two cottages and she lives next door to her brother Bill Barrow. It's just round the corner from where I live, and it's really lovely. Bertha entertains the pensioners and church ladies groups by reciting and yodelling very well. She's marvellous for her age, as indeed her brother is as well. Just one point about the Stonefold Maypole – it does still exist. My own two daughters used to go out with the Sunday School dancing round the Maypole to raise money for Stonefold Church, and I'm glad to say that the tradition it still being carried on by the children of Stonefold.

The two 'Jims' and their walls!

THE art of dry stone walling is very little known in some areas, although it's been practised for centuries. Quite often the tricks of the trade have been handed down from father to son, and this ancient art is very skilled and valuable. One would think that with all the fields about, there would be much more use for this type of wall, but I'm told that fencing like wood, barbed wire or even hawthorn hedges are more in use, because they are less costly and don't need as much maintenance. I was surprised to find in Rising Bridge, though, two men who are both retired stonemasons – Benny Barnes and Bill Hodgkinson; and more importantly, two men, a father and son, who still practise the art of dry stone walling. I was determined to seek them out and ask them about their trade.

Thus it was then, that on a lovely Sunday in May, I walked from Rising Bridge up through Stonefold Village, past Black Moss Farm and took the path up to Hen Heads Farm, to meet *young* Jim Hardicker, master of the art of dry stone walling. As I walked through the yard dozens of hens appeared as if by magic – probably thinking I was going to feed them, but they were unlucky for once. Mary, Jim's wife, was busy cleaning eggs in the kitchen and she very kindly made me coffee whilst I waited to talk to her husband.

When Jim did arrive, he was every inch the typical farmer in boots, tweed jacket and pants and grey bob cap. Jim said they'd been at Hen Heads Farm for almost 35 years and that yes, his father, now

81, had taught him how to repair and build dry stone walls. I asked Jim if his father – also a Jim – had learnt the trade from his father before him.

'No – it was just that at Ribchester, before we came here, there were a lot of thorn hedges, so we just picked up how to wall as we went along, and we learned by experience as you do in many trades.'

I asked young Jim to tell me how he repaired a dry stone wall and certainly he seemed to know the art very well.

'Well,' he said: 'The foundation, depending on ground conditions needs to be four to six inches deep, twenty to twenty-four inches wide as well. You then start with the big stones at the bottom, and as you build up, the wall narrows to about nine inches at the top. After about two feet height, you put flat stones in at intervals as you build – all field walls are double thickness bonded together with small stones put in the middle. The small stones fill the joints and prevents them rocking and also stops the wind from getting through. You just keep on building the walls and practising so over the years you get better at it. It's just like putting a giant jigsaw puzzle together and making the stones fit. It's like anything else – the more you do, the easier it becomes.'

'Where do you get the stones from, do you scour the moors for them or take them up with you?' I asked.

'Generally, at the moment, we use what's there, say an old wall or a building that's derelict, or

sometimes we buy a load from somewhere else.'

And so I listened to Jim about his work and was fascinated by what he told me. Jim and his father are so good at their job, in fact, that Rossendale Groundwork Trust have included him in a video they have made for craft purposes and it was interesting to see them at work on their own farm walls.

'Our farm is about 190 acres at the moment – not very big really, but I do building work as well so I've plenty to do,' Jim told me. 'We've had some rough winters up here though. I remember one year when the road was only open two days in seven weeks! We'd to dig sheep out of snowdrifts – three weeks were the longest some were buried, yet they were still alive. At the moment we've about two hundred sheep, two dogs, five hundred hens and half a dozen cats. We've also wild geese nesting at the moment; we get a lot of wild birds including partridge.

The old Stonefold Mill was running for a few years after we came to Hen Heads. We've about 4-5 miles of dry stone wall to maintain. When a wall's been repaired it should last for the better part of a hundred years, but a lot depends on the stone used. Haslingden is the highest town above sea level in Lancashire and we get a lot of winds up here. We've free range hens as well, and farm work is interesting – we don't know what's going to turn-up next. We get a lot of pleasure out of our work but the animals always come first. There's great pleasure in seeing the wild flowers, herbs, stoats, weasels and the occasional fox. The fresh air and work keeps us healthy, and with our open fire we are comfortable, we can burn all the rubbish except tins – we bury tins.'

Certainly, sat round the fire talking to young Jim and watching Mary wash and grade eggs was most relaxing and I envied them their peaceful existence. Physically hard work – but very satisfying and not at all stressful. Mary still has a huge wide rack in her farm kitchen, made for them as a wedding present. She is a Stonefold Village girl herself and is very suited to the country life she lives.

Jim told me that years ago he'd been given two pieces of advice which he's always remembered:
1) Young sheep may die – old ones will, so always keep young sheep.
2) If you don't show someone else how to do the job, then you'll have to do it all yourself.

'I can't remember who told me,' said Jim, 'but I've always tried to work accordingly.

Normally I only did the farm part time as I did a lot of building work as well; slating, roofing, tiling etc. I enjoyed it all very much though. Mi dad ran the farm before, whilst I did the building work, but now he just helps when he can and I run the farm.'

'What's the origin of the name – Hen Heads Farm?' I asked.

'Well, there were two explanations; one said that Hen Heads Farm was a farm originally from Sawley Abbey where it was called 'The End of the Heads Farm'; the other one was that it was the 'Head' of the river and this farm was where the river divided. The 'hens' part was the game birds up here – grouse, partridge etc. We're up near Mitchells Reservoir and there's quite a lot of birds up there now.'

'I remember the pub – the George and Dragon – at Stonefold Village before it closed down, and the two fire beaters at the mill were Danny Heaton and Sam Shilliday. A lot of young people today are taking an interest in the old crafts now.'

Mary said she used to work as a weaver, but much preferred to work on the farm and take charge of five hundred hens:

'They're all very tame but tend to lay in some peculiar places sometimes and I have to search for the nests,' she added.

I thanked Jim and Mary for their interesting talk and walked back to Stonefold Village to talk to 'Old Jim' who lives there. Mary gave me some lovely free range eggs to take home with me and when I used them for baking you could see the rich, yellow yolks which make lovely cakes.

'Old Jim' – now 81 – James William and commonly known as 'Jim Willie', lives in a little house in Stonefold Village and has done for some time, but he still goes up to Hen Heads Farm to help his son with the dry stone walling.

'Well, a learned dry stone walling up here on mi own – a had to because allut walls wer down an I'd to ged em up agen. I've done walling up here on the moors, at our farm and at Black Moss nearby. I come from Clayton-le-Dale originally an we weren't weel off at all. Mi father died when I wer six and mi mother when I wer fourteen, so I had to go into service. I went wi Bill Dent at Samlesbury – he'd four hundred head o' cattle when he deed had Bill.

I wer supposed to retire when I cum up here, but a taught mi son dry walling instead. I had a full time job without the walls belonging to t' farm.

The Stonefold Mill wer working when a came up, but I've sin some changes up here though – id used to be all horses. But it wer all blue stone then, like thi mended the roads with, an allut dust used to fly over t' houses – thi wer full o' dust an white in summertime.

We had a nephew called John as had polio. He wer in a wheelchair, but he still managed to do joinering work and other good things, but he couldn't push a wheelbarra – he'd irons up his legs you see.

We got more snow i Rising Bridge than anywheer else because of the warm smoke rising when the mills wer working. One man told me you could only see across the valley when it wer 'Wakes Weeks.' The stone walls wer full o' soot and all black, when we started to pull 'em down, but they're cleaner now. Stonefold Mill wer well built – that's partly wer John Holden has 'is bungalow now. Withers Grove Farm wer added onto our farm later. One day a gable end cum down as well.

I likes to live on mi own an eat Lancashire food – there's nowt wrong wi some good Lancashire Hotpot - 'lob scouse' wi call it, it's better digested than some food today. We used to use all the old fashioned remedies fer sprains etc., like Belladonna, knitbone an herbs. Mi mother had all th' old remedies so we seldom had the doctor.

A learned stone walling like many farmers – by their bosses. We got most of our stone from the quarry and what was lying around, horses could bring it up to the fields.

I wanted to keep sheep when a first cum up Rising Bridge but neighbours weren't keen. Well, mi son has sheep now and it's fine. I'm a poor do at walling now and it's a job getting about the stone when yer helping, but a do mi best! I'm not so much damned good now, though. Mary said they'd bin troubled wi rustlers up on t' moors these last few years. Fancy! – Rustlers in Rising Bridge!'

It gave me much food for thought as I left old Jim and walked home across the moors and down Northfield Road. Young Jim was still hard at work picking up stones from the field before they were mowed. He does this to prevent the machinery being damaged, but it's back breaking over a long period. My admiration for the Hardicker family grew as I thought of all the wide variety of work that they do so well – and particularly keeping the art of dry stone walling alive. With the fresh moorland air and Mary's good, homely, Lancashire food, they should enjoy their hard but stress-free way of life for many years to come. I certainly hope so.

Margaret Trippier
of
Haslingden

Margaret Trippier – a true 'Lancashire Lass'

'I wer born in Haslingden in Market Street South in 1916. Mi father was in the 'Med' when I wer born and I wer three years old before he saw me. I went to St. James' Parish Church School.; the headmaster wer a Mr. Howarth. I used to get the cane fer talking and not knowing mi lessons. When I wer ten, we went to live at Windy Harbour Farm on the Grane Road. Later I went to the council school in Ryefield Avenue, then we moved to Roundhill in Rising Bridge, where I went to the Wesley School which I liked very much. When I left school, I went weaving with mi father. I wer allus in trouble wi mi father fer not watching mi work; but I didn't like weaving. During the war I went to work on the buses an we had to have a test in mental arithmetic; I passed in that so I wer on the buses in Haslingden fer a few years. Some of the men wer former tram drivers an the men used to say: 'Cleyn thi clogs, put plenty o' polish on it, watter proof 'em!'

I wer taught by an older man, who showed mi all the 'tricks of the trade'. I wer told to keep the money in mi hand until I'd given the passengers their change. I really loved every minute of it. But I had to go back to weaving parachute cloth at Grane Manufacturing Company; it broke mi heart! As soon as the essential work order wer stopped I went to work on Accrington buses. We went to Whalley, Blackburn, Burnley, all over the area. Then after about four years I went back on Haslingden buses. When I wer on the Accrington route I remember a time when there wer a long queue in St. James' Street, waiting fer the bus. One man wer carrying a big roll of oilcloth and I told this passenger he'd have to stand on the platform to stop the oilcloth from rolling off. The man wer fed up standing and he went upstairs fer a smoke. I had mi fares to collect, so I couldn't watch his oilcloth. When we went round a corner it rolled off the bus. The passenger told mi later that he couldn't find it so he went and got drunk!

I thought on one occasion I wer going to be a midwife. A girl on the bus started 'with her pains' and she had a young child with her as well! This wer coming down from Bacup. Anyway I put her off at a shop and told her to go in there and ask fer help. A midwife got on the bus at the next stop and when I told her she went back to the girl. Apparently she wer one of this midwife's patients!'

How did you manage in the snow and frost?

'We used to beg ashes from the houses to put under the bus wheels. When mi father died I went to work at 'Shepherds Timber'. I wer 'spot welding', then I worked in the joinery department. One day I wer left to finish painting a greenhouse – but I got the colour wrong and had to paint it again.'

Tell me about the entertainment in Haslingden

'Oh it wer great! We went to the Public Hall, dancing, also the Ambulance Hall, the Labour Hall and all the Sunday Schools. There wer also the Palace and Empire picture places. We had soldiers billeting in Haslingden who came to the dances so we had a good time; we'd plenty o' partners in Haslingden.

We had an outdoor market in Haslingden, which wer very popular; it wer down Deardengate. There wer all kinds of stalls selling vegetables and fruit etc. There wer one stall that sold toffee which wer very popular. I used to be in all the Sunday School concerts when I wer young. I like the Lancashire dialect which I still recite at pensioners' clubs and socials.'

Did you wear clogs?

'Oh yes! I got a pair when I left school and I had them fer ten years. Mi dad had said: "Get 'em big enough," and I did, so thi lasted mi a long time.'

Where did you spend your holidays?

'Blackpool mostly. We danced on the pier and in the Winter Gardens and Tower Ballrooms. We went to the Isle O' Man, only once.'

Now you've retired, what do you do?

'Oh, I'm never in! I go to the Haslingden Pensioners every Tuesday afternoon at the Public Hall. Wednesday is the over-sixties club at Greenfield Gardens; I'm a committee member there. I've also joined the Mothers Union at St. James'. The Co-op Guild Group meet every Tuesday night and we enjoy life there. Yes, I do a lot of things.'

Housework must have changed over the years.

'Oh it has. I just take mi laundry to the launderette now and it's washed 'n' dried while you wait.'

How do you like this little flat after always living in a house?

'Oh I've got used to it; I like it! We have bingo twice a week in the Social Room etc.'

When you worked on the buses at first, did you walk to work?

'Yes, and one shift started at 5 am. It went to a mill thi called 'Rag Shop' outside Rawtenstall. Mi later years wer spent as a domestic in Rawtenstall General Hospital, I enjoyed that too. I wer there about ten years in all.'

Are you connected with David Trippier, the M.P. for Rossendale and Darwen?

'If I am it's a long way back!'

I remember being at a dance where there wer one girl whose mother was a dressmaker, she always wore lovely clothes. I asked her about school. She wer at the same school as me but she said she didn't like school and didn't want to know about it. I wer allus very happy at school.

Mi grandmother lived in Dough Lane; it wer named after the Dough Times when an employer couldn't afford to pay his workers so he gave them flour instead. The old lady didn't go to school because her parents couldn't pay the penny fee; so she couldn't learn to read. She didn't learn until her husband taught her by reading newspapers.

'Edgar fra' t' Grane' wer a real character – he wer a rag and bone man but he only carried a sack. He lived at Heaps' Clough wi his sister Alice. Edgar got married and as we wer going home from school we saw these lines wi babies' nappies hanging out. We wer laughing – then Edgar came out and wer running us up road. He got married but we never saw his wife or children (if he had any, that is!)'

Margaret is still a very lively person and very good at reciting Lancashire dialect. She's a friendly, happy person who is also good fun.

Deardengate, Haslingden, in 1913

A crowded scene in Haslingden's market place around the turn of the century

Ted Berry
former 'marine dealer' in Haslingden

'I was born in Haslingden and went to St. James's School. When I left at fourteen I joined mi father in the marine dealers yard [rag men] where we dealt in scrap metal and rags etc. I did that for about 45 years. I then had a spell at Nori Brick Yard in Clayton-le-Moors, but after contracting bronchitis I had to leave. Mi father was originally a weaver at Spring Vale Mill in Haslingden. Mi grandmother, Annie Berry, was a good worker though, she knew a lot about the marine dealer's business. She was very fond of

jewellery too; rings and such! Mi father delivered coal in half-hundredweight bags. He also took coke out to bakers for their ovens. He got the coke from the old gas works on Grane Road [now demolished]. We had many street rounds in the marine dealer's business and we collected rags and scrap between Rawtenstall and Accrington and we picked up many a bargain. We gave donkey stones and 'flying birds' on a stick in exchange for the rags or jam jars. We got loads and loads in them days. We also had bundles of

firewood to exchange. We made the rags into bundles and a man came from Bradford to buy them. People often say that those were the 'bad old days' but I think they were good days; they were happy days at least. Those same donkey stones cost 30p today – when you can get them, that is. We used to buy them by the wagon load from a Burnley firm called Halstead, I think. Mi grandmother paid a penny for a one pound jam jar and tuppence for a two pound jar, she wer a good businesswoman, she wer! A jam-making firm bought the jars from us; they cleaned and sterilized them and re-used them.

The Deardengate Market in Haslingden was very popular. The stalls used to fill the street between Church Street and Regent Street. The fish market was in front of the Empire [now a Bingo Hall]. There were also 'Quack Stalls', where 'miracle cures' were sold. Church

Street had plenty of cook shops – homemade pies, cakes, bread etc. They sold potato pie dinners all homemade fer about 1/9d [9p] . You could have peas, pudding or pie, college pudding or rice with a cake and a pint of tea just fer that. I used to go to thi chip shop with a tin basin fer a 'tuppeny mixture' [chips and peas] and a meat pie with mint sauce on. That chip shop was Fred Wilson's.

The 'knocker up' used to tap on the bedroom windows with a large cane to get the mill workers up for their 6am start. I also remember the lamplighter who had a long pole with a hook on the end with which he pulled on the gas. The taper at the other side lighted it. The ponies we used on the rag carts were shod at Carr Mill Street. The blacksmith wer Jimmy Marsden. There was another blacksmith on Grane Road.

I was always fond of fairgrounds and circuses; mi father and I used to go to carnivals a lot – all over the area. He used to ride his 'boneshaker' [penny farthing] bike and his 'kangaroo' bike. His name was George Berry – 'The Carnival King'. They called him that because he rode his bikes in the carnivals all over Lancashire and everybody knew him. I know a lot of old Romanies and I went to Appleby one year to their meeting, it was very interesting.

I remember mi mother and father working at Spring Vale Mill. They finished at 5.30pm and they'd be lucky to earn £3 a week for two of them. I've never seen a 'rag round' here at Haslingden for at least a year. I used to collect the stuff that was left unsold after a jumble sale. The fair used to be held on Marsden Square and we went when we could. Haslingden has changed over the years though. I've never been a drinker but I do like a cigarette.'

Ted still remembers the 'good old days' of the rag trade; he's got plenty of relics left that he treasures too!

Textile Mills in Haslingden

Industrial Mill – now Holland's Pies
Rising Bridge Mill
Stonefold Mill
Hazel Mill – Rothwell, Worsley's
Clough End Mill – Worsley's
Duckworth Clough Mill – Worsley's
Carr Mill
Albert Mill – Anderton & Halstead
Britannia Mill
Vale Mill
Robinson's Union Mill
Bottom Oak Brow Mill
Commercial Mill
Vine Grove Mill
Grove Mill
Lambert's Carr Mill – J. Whittaker's
Fountains Mill (Scarpa) – J. Whittaker's
Hargreaves Street Mill – Rothwell, Worsley
Carr Parker's Charles Lane Mill
Waterside Mill (John Warburton's) – Higham's
Spring Vale Mill – J. Whittaker's
Plantation Mill (Nickey's)
Hutch Bank Mill (Blown up)
Grane Road Mill (Birtwistle's) – Tattersall's
Home Spring Mill – J. Whittaker's
Higher Mill (woollen) – Hardman's
Grane Mill (Longshoot)
Higher Mill – L. Whittaker's
Park Mill – Birtwistle's
Barlow's Mill (Sunny Bank)
Flash Mill
Middle Mill – now Air Tours
Porritt's (woollen)
Albion Mill – J. Whittaker's
Syke Mill (Slater's)
Sykeside Mill – Higham's
Lockgate Mill
Ewood Bridge Mill – Anderton & Halstead
Bowl Alley – Porritt's (formerly Turner's)
Irwell Vale Mill (Aitken's)

Only Grane Road Mill and Sykeside Mill are still in production.

List supplied by Mr. George Wellock of Haslingden.

Did you know?

That the Empire Bingo Hall (ex cinema) was originally the Parish Church vicarage.

That the road through Sherfin (King's Highway) and Stonefold is an old stage coach road. The stage stop was the White Horse Inn (demolished just before the war) at the top of Church Street.

That two toll houses are still in existence: Jumble Holes Bar House (just above the Farmer's Glory) and Kirk Hill Bar House (just above where I live). There were others, now demolished, at the top of Hud Hey and the bottom of Bury Road.

That there are old weavers' cottages behind the British Legion.

That there has been a church on the St. James's site since 1280.

That underneath the ground in Haslingden centre there are huge water tanks.

That in the First World War a Zeppelin came over to bomb Holden Wood (it was then Nobel's Gunpowder). It missed and dropped its bombs near Holcombe. All the inhabitants of Grane stood in the streets to watch; I was in my mother's arms.

Of the Irish Patriot Michael Davitt's association with Haslingden. He lost an arm in a cotton mill. There are two memorials to Michael Davitt still in Haslingden, but he is buried in Straid, Southern Ireland. There is also a Davitt Close.

Thanks to George Wellock for his information.

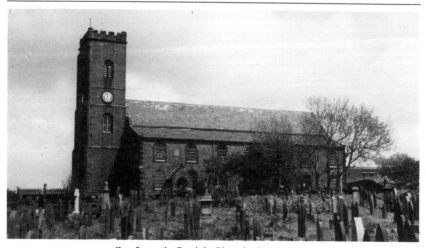

St. James's Parish Church, Haslingden

Agnes Howarth

Entertainer, charity worker and pensioners' 'champion'

Start at the beginning Agnes, where were you born?

'In Blackburn at Larkhill. There were quite a number of theatres in the area then and my mother often took us to see the shows: so we knew Gracie Fields and Charlie Chaplin and other well known stars who came to the Grand and the Theatre Royal. We were always connected with the theatre and interested in it. At one time my mother 'ran away' with Gracie Fields and Charlie Chaplin because she was so keen on theatrical work. My mother's father was one of the old fashioned, strict, Victorian parents and he dragged my mother back. No way was a child of his going to be on the stage! My grandfather was a refugee from the potato famine in Ireland. My father's family were English and in business, but he lost all his money in the slump. My mother took part in the church concerts and I had singing and dancing lessons as a child, so you can see why I'm keen on entertaining and raising money for charity when possible.

At one stage we had a childrens' choir in Blackburn; this was during the depression in the 1930s. There was a 'Cotton Week' held in Blackburn, at King George's Hall and stalls were set up displaying anything appertaining to cotton.

The children were all dressed in white and sang every night, this was to promote the cotton trade. This was about the same time that a children's choir from Manchester recorded the song: 'Nymphs and Shepherds'.

I worked at the Imperial Mill in Blackburn during the war and I lost my finger and thumb; I trapped them in a machine! This meant that I'd to find another job and I was sent to the Shirley Institute in Manchester to train to be a yarn tester. From there I went to Manchester University and I eventually became quality controller for the Lancashire Cotton Company. After my husband came home from the war, where he'd had a rough time as a prisoner in Germany, we moved to Helmshore. So then I had to look for another job. I applied and got a job as quality controller for four or five mills in a group, who set up their own laboratory for the John Warburton Organisation. I spent fifteen happy years in that job, it was very interesting. Later I felt like I wanted to 'stretch myself' and ended up at Platt Saco Lowell (formerly Howard and Bulloughs) We invented the machines that put everybody out of work but we didn't know what we were doing at the time! As usual we were bought out by the Americans and we were all made redundant. All our patents were taken to Georgia in the U.S.A. and Georgia is now thriving on our brain work whilst Lancashire is left with nothing!

I became interested in the politics of the Liberal Party. A lady, Gertrude Warburton, lived in Haslingden; she was very well respected in the town. She lived in Wellbank and was a govenor of the Catholic school etc. She had been elected to the council without much opposition and had been on quite a while. Well, democracy was what we'd fought the war for and so I thought that it was time that this lady fought for her seat. I put up against her as a Liberal. Well,

all kinds of people came and asked me not to put up against Mrs Warburton; although it was assumed that no-one else could win that seat. However, I had a lot of support and in this context Councillor Butterworth came down to the works (he used to be the transport manager at John Warburtons). He asked me to withdraw because the Tory Party didn't want to lose the seat. Anyway, I didn't withdraw, I stood against her and I lost by a narrow margin; but I enjoyed the whole contest!

I joined the Haslingden Arts Club and we put on plays and all kinds of shows which we had great fun doing. My theatrical background was very useful here. It was a great organisation which led me into Rossendale Amateurs, where I took part in many musical shows. Eventually though, I felt it was time I stepped aside to allow the young people in, so I retired. I then began to do concerts for charity. The Friends of Rossendale Hospital wanted to buy an ultra-sound machine for the maternity unit. We needed £16,000 but only had £4,000; so the administrator said we could have the machine for £10,000. 'Get it and I'll give you a room to put it in and you can pay for it afterwards,' he said. So we accepted the machine and had it put in the clinic at Brinbella where it still is. My husband Bill and myself had raised £50 in a raffle; but the winner didn't claim his prize so we decided to raffle the prize again; it was a doll. However after selling £20 worth of tickets, we were stopped by an official who thought it was wrong to re-raffle. He refused to take the £20, so we booked a room at the Haslingden Public Hall and put an 'Old Time Music Show' on, making a profit of £400. We were putting on shows for twelve months at the end of which we only owed £400 for the ultra-sound machine. Finally we raised over the £10,000 needed and the hospital authorities were really

pleased with us. We had money left over, and discovering that some hospital beds badly needed replacing, we put out another appeal. We put on another concert in Haslingden and all the surrounding districts, and by the end of two years we'd replaced 130 beds. We were called the 'Good Neighbour Concert Party' and from there we went all over giving concerts and became the public relations for the hospitals. We later became involved in the Guide Dogs for the Blind organisation, and we sponsored a dog called Sherry which meant raising £1,000. We got children together in the Sports Hall and put on a concert which was a great success. Then we went out to various clubs and pensioners' groups and we were given many donations. At the end of twelve months the children had raised over £600. We 'made' this up to £1,000 to sponsor Sherry and his picture was taken and given to the children. I still work for the Guide Dogs Committee and am president of the Haslingden and Helmshore Old Age Pensioners. I'd retired once and was going to sit back and enjoy miself but ended up as president, which I still am after ten years!'

Can you tell me anything about the revival of the Street Market in Deardengate?

'Well, Sheila Oldham decided to have a street market again, with charity stalls. I was on the first stall for the Friends of the Hospital and it poured down! This was 1980, the year we were fund-raising for the ultra-sound machine. It's been held every year since though and been very successful.'

Agnes and Bill haven't had easy lives, but they've overcome all their difficulties to become champion workers for charitable causes. The 'Good Neighbours' are still thriving, and if any charity needs a helping hand, Agnes is always there!

Joe and Agnes Gill on their cooked meat stall in Rawtenstall Market

Mr. Joe Gill

Trader on Rawtenstall Market
for over fifty years

Where were you born?

'Leigh Farm, Rawtenstall, up Hurst Lane. I'm one of ten children – eight sisters and a brother. I lived up there until I was 26, then the farm had to be demolished so that the cemetery could be extended. We came to live in Crankshaw Street, in Rawtenstall, then we went to live in Burnley Road. I was working on the market all this time.

I went to St. James-the-Less School till I was fourteen. Then I started work at 'Melias' (the grocers) in Bank Street, the manager was John Ramsden. I was then made manager of the Haslingden branch of Melias on the main road. This was well before the war and it's now Schofield's confectioners. I started on the market at Haslingden with a stall for Melias, but I was coming up to 21 and wanting more money so I started on mi own. Melias sold bacon, cooked meats and grocery etc. I started with groceries and cooked meats as well as bacon and anything else people wanted.

Saturday was the busiest day of the week. There were a lot of Co-op shops in Haslingden at that time, so we'd plenty of competition. Melias eventually gave up on the market stall and so I carried on. I used to do Haslingden on Tuesdays; Bacup on a Wednesday; Rawtenstall Thursday; Waterfoot on Friday and Rawtenstall on Saturday.'

Where did Melias originate?

'From Liverpool. This was when the multiple shops were expanding. However, when people had to register just before the war they went to the nearest shop, so the market trade started to decline. Bacup was the busiest market and having a food stall meant being covered-in on three sides for reasons of hygiene. I got my bacon from a Danish wholesaler in Manchester called Neilson. I dealt with Hitchens as well, they were wholesale grocers on Hyndburn Road in Accrington.

War broke out when I was working on the market and I was called up with the 'twenty-sixes'. I obtained an extension of leave so that I could teach my wife and sister the business so they could keep it going in Rawtenstall whilst I was away. I went into the army in January 1941 and I was away four and a half years, but my wife and sister kept the business going. When I came home I couldn't get my licences back for the other markets. There was an off-licence in South Street, Rawtenstall, which I took. We were living in Bacup at the time, but we moved to

Rawtenstall. I had two days on Rawtenstall market and the off-licence. Six weeks before I was demobbed, I received a telegram from the police: 'Come home at once, business burned down.'

I got home at midnight and found that the market stall had been completely destroyed. The authorities had to find us a place in the town because we had registered customers who couldn't get supplies anywhere else. We were found a shop in Bank Street, but later that year we came back to the market. The market inspector at that time was a man called Richmond who had also been in the army. The open market had been covered-in so we started a second time after the fire.'

Rawtenstall Market before the fire in the 1940s

How did you manage to get your supplies again?

'Well, we got enough to supply our own customers. The day of the fire we'd just had a week's delivery. Things were getting back to normal then but goods were not easy to get. We got the stall on Rawtenstall Market where I stayed till I retired.'

Did the Asda Supermarket hit your trade?

'Well, I thought it brought more people into the town. We got more on the market, although I'm not saying everyone was happy about it, but it did me no harm. We had a very good regular trade – families came, one generation after another for years and years.'

What were the most popular goods?

'Well I had the best trade in bacon, cooked meats and cheeses, but I had the groceries if anyone wanted them. I sold an enormous amount of bacon and cheese; cooked meat was home-cooked in Rawtenstall. Hail, rain or snow, our regular customers came, especially the

elderly ones. We got really friendly with them; they liked to chat as well as buy. There used to be a toffee stall and the toffee was made on the stall. Another man sold nothing but celery at one time.

There were several greengrocery stalls; fancy goods; women's clothes; also a butcher etc. Slinger's butchers from Accrington had a stall on Rawtenstall Market. Billy Ainsworth and his wife had the market cafe for many years as well.'

Agnes Gill – Joe's wife and helpmate in the business.

Where were you born and bred?

'Turn Village. My grandfather owned Scout Pit up there. When he was killed, the pit was closed and we had to move to Bacup. I went to a school at Turn before we moved to Bacup. We then went to Sharneyford School, and my father was the colliery fireman at Hargreaves' Pit. We stayed there till the pit closed, then mi father then went to work near Todmorden at a sanitary and pipe works. Eventually, we moved to this shop in Rawtenstall. We later moved to Rose Bank as my

children were growing up, and we stayed there for over twenty years.'

Did you work on the market?

'Yes, after we got married in 1940. My first child was born in 1946 so I was at home after that. I worked all the war years when Joe was in the army. There wasn't much money in the business though, we only got the bare rations for our customers, but at least it kept it going until mi husband came back. After the fire it was a few years before I came back into the business, in the 1950s then.'

How do you see the changes from a woman's point of view?

'Well it seems to get busier; more people, more money. I think people were so deprived at one time that, once they got the money business has improved. We were the 'old fashioned' type of family grocer who gave a personal service so we kept all our customers even when Asda opened. My husband's mother bought him a set of white overalls and aprons when we got married. People were very practical in our early days, not like today.

We made a lot of new friends when we were on the market. Food's not the same today though I think, the food given to the animals is not always pure. We were told that milk and butter and eggs were the foods to give to growing children; now we are told that these foods are unhealthy. It's two years since I finished on the market.'

How did you cope with the bad winters?

'Well I do think that when you're standing outside you do get acclimatised to it to a certain extent, and after a while, you don't notice the cold the same.'

Altogether, Joe and Agnes did 52 years on Rawtenstall Market, and certainly they were always famous for their home-cooked meats and brawn etc. Joe isn't as well as he used to be, but Agnes looks after him well, and he looks back on his market days with nostalgia.

Vincent Cryne
retired blacksmith and Master Farrier

IN the heart of Rawtenstall, I was lucky to discover a retired Master Farrier, Vincent Thomas Cryne. He'd been active all his life until just a few years ago, and to say he's had such a hard job, looked remarkably well. Vincent is one of the few remaining blacksmiths alive, and he's also the proud possessor of a certificate admitting him to the trade of Master Farrier in 1938, a fact of which he's very proud.

'I was born in Ramsbottom and we then moved to Summerseat when I was eight years old, and mi father had a public house called, 'The Weavers Arms'. This closed later and we moved to Bury where we had a shop. I always did a lot of singing there and I was a boy soprano. I've lots of cuttings from the *Bury Times* about this. Then I became apprenticed to a blacksmith which is a long cry from a singer! I was apprenticed to Richard Ashcroft who had his place at Elton at t'back of the Eagle and Child pub. He wer a champion blacksmith actually and very good at his trade. We used to shoe all the big shire horses of J. & W. Whewell who had the champion shire horses of England fer years and years. They had a chemical works in Radcliffe, and also a stud farm up Unsworth with all kinds of horses – 120 in all. Later he moved house to Heaton with big stalls and horses there, and after work, we'd to go and shoe fer him then. I'd to get on mi push bike and cycle up there wi mi tools after work.'

How old were you when you did this?

'Oh not very old – in mi teens. I'd always been very fragile actually, very tiny, but I'd still to get 'on mi bike' with all these heavy tools. Billy Whewell had all the horses and his brother Joe ran the chemical works. Sometimes I'd shoe a horse and then walk back to Radcliffe with it. Joe always asked me in the office when I did this, and I'd sing 'Danny Boy' and the 'Rose of Tralee' fer him. Mi wage then wer 7/6d per week, and if I sang both songs then he gave me five shillings, so I wer glad to take the horses back.'

Everybody expects blacksmiths to be massive and strong yet you say you were delicate. How did you manage such heavy work, and was it your idea to be apprenticed to a blacksmith?

'Well yes, everybody thinks we're big and strong, but not all blacksmiths are built like that. When I left school, work wer hard to get and mi dad said: 'There's two jobs here – one fer a painter and one fer a blacksmith. Painters get lead poisoning which won't be good fer yer singing, so you'd better be a blacksmith. Blacksmiths are the second longest livers to farmers, so you'll be guaranteed a long life and an interesting one' – and it always has been fer me.'

Had Mr. Ashcroft only you working for him?

'No, we did general work as well, so he'd another man called Wilfred Emmerson who wer a right good bloke as well. We had the anvil and the forge as usual, and we worked well together; never a wrong word. When the war came I volunteered and do you know, I wer sent to Lumb Mill at Irwell Vale because the Duke of Lancaster's Yeomen wer there with all ther horses and thi wer short of a blacksmith so I wer sent to them. I stayed with them until 1941, when thi mechanised things and I wer sent with the horses to Derby Racecourse. Later I wer moved to Ashbourne and then Nottingham Racecourse fer the stables. Afterwards, thi decided thi didn't want the horses and sold them off, and the top horse brought £33 on Derby Market. Thi wer sold on the condition that the army could have them back if thi wanted, and twelve months later thi wanted them back fer the jungle in Burmah and in Italy fer the mountains. I worked every day; I never missed a day without some shoeing.'

But if you were delicate – how did you manage?.

'Well, as I used all mi muscles, I became stronger. At one time I wer fifteen stone – I wer massive'.

You must have a feeling for the animals though?

'Yes I did. It's funny, but I'm a Catholic and we had to have a confirmation name and the nuns suggested Francis – like St. Francis with the birds etc. I've often thought since it's worked in wi mi job, and I've bin called out to troublesome horses but they've always let mi shoe 'em. A once went to shoe a small pony – and when they're small they're awkward to get round and under. He'd had it to two smiths before and thi couldn't do it, so he called me and I said I would. It wer in a field wi another, so a told him to tie it up to the other one. Now I'd half a pound of treacle toffee in mi pocket and thi both got some, so I'd no bother at all, and a shoed it in three quarters of an hour. His grandson told mi later he swore I'd drugged it wi treacle toffee! I always remember that, but you see I'm always quiet wi 'em and don't shout at 'em at all. At the end of the war a finished up as a Farrier Sergeant in the R.A.U.C and I actually shod Mussolini's charger.'

How did that come about?

'All the captured animals were sent to a camp in Italy, and I'd about twenty Italian blacksmiths working fer mi as well as the English ones.

One morning, all the Italians wer making a commotion and all I could hear was: '*Viva Mussolini's cavallo*'. Mussolini's horse was there with the others, and I'd to shoe it. We wer kept really busy there shoeing horses, and at the barracks twice a month, a boat-load of mules came from India and the Middle East to be used as pack mules so we'd to do them as well. The mules from Argentina wer much bigger and used as ambulances. They could carry a man each side on a stretcher and come down a mountainside without banging the men; they wer very intelligent animals. The mules also could tell where mines wer, and the drivers would send one in front and hold it's tail and it would pick its way through the path or field. It was very seldom a mule trod on the mine, they could sense where the ground had been disturbed.

When I was demobbed, Mr. Ashcroft had retired and the other man had taken over the business and he had an apprentice already. Ther wasn't enough work fer three of us, as the farmers wer using vans and the coal merchants' lorries, so I decided to learn welding at Bury nightschool. I kept looking fer work, then the manager at Porritt and Spencers in Helmshore (he was called John Batley) he told me their blacksmith was retiring in eighteen months' time, so he sent fer me and I stayed ther until I'd finished mi time. I was doing general blacksmithing, but did shoeing fer Harry Haworth who carted rubbish to the tips. Ther wer also a pony on the Porritt estate that the children rode, and the funny thing about it wer the chauffeur's wife used to give it two 'Churchmans Number 1' cigarettes each day and it ate them! Another peculiar thing about this donkey; Mr Cullen the Estate Agent looked after her, and he came down one day and said: 'I'm sorry to tell you, but Jenny (the donkey) died last night after 33 years.' And do you know, only a week later, Mr.

Cullen himself died as well, it wer uncanny really.

After that, a carried on blacksmithing, and mi grandson Ian had a pony – he really took to horses, and a used to shoe fer him as well, but I'd a good job'. (There his wife Jean added: 'I'm not joking, he carried on shoeing horses till he wer seventy years old'.) 'But I must emphasise this; it's come full circle, because when I served mi time as a blacksmith up to being called up, fer every riding horse which only the gentry had in those days, there must have bin twenty cart horses, and today it's the other way round. For every shire horse now, there must be twenty or thirty riding horses or ponies.'

This is fascinating – let me see your certificate please. [Vincent showed me his certificate of registration which is now fifty years old.]

'Mi boss wer very particular, and whether it wer a riding horse or a rag-tatter's donkey, it had to be shod properly, and he insisted on this. I've a lovely silver horseshoe here which I made Jean when we wer married, a made it at the nightschool fer her.'

You must always keep it the right way up though to keep the good luck in, isn't that right Jean?

'Yes that's right,' said Jean, then Vincent added that the blacksmith was always known as: 'King of the Tradesmen'. 'Thi always had tassels on ther leather aprons to denote rank, because the blacksmith made all the tools fer the other tradesmen. The blacksmith was always important in the villages as well as the towns because he made tools, brackets and all other kinds of useful things. I'll tell you about our Ian's pony though; fer it's size, it wer a better horse than Red Rum, because it

Vincent and Jean Cryne proudly display his certificate of registration as a member of the Worshipful Company of Farriers

used to enter its own classes in the pony class and win that, then it would go in with the horses and beat them as well. Thi used to be fed up o' seeing it, they'd no chance when he wer on the scene.'

There's very few blacksmiths left now; is your grandson not interested in taking it up?

'Well no, I wanted him to, but he didn't want to do it. He allus did riding though and loved horses. We went to Leverhulme Park at Bolton, and it wer the only pony to win the cup three times.'

Are you still singing?

'Oh yes, I go to entertain the old people as much as I can, especially at Christmas, and I compere the parties as well sometimes.'

I'll bet you've always been healthy too?

'Yes. Ever since I left school up to finishing work, I've only had three days off work, and that was with lumbago, it's a very healthy life! (Jean added: 'He's always bin healthy up to being seventy when he had a slight heart attack, and thi told him it wer the last pony he'd ever shoe'.)

'Whewell's at Radcliffe wer the leading people in the country with shire horses, and thi had five or six teams which took the chemicals out to Manchester and Blackburn etc. One horse that stands out in my memory was 'Kerry, Cornish Maid', and it weighed 1 ton 5cwt (25cwt) and it won the championship of Great Britain three times on the run, and I'd to shoe it.'

Did you ever harm yourself or have accidents?

'A few, but you'd not to bother about that! First morning a went to work me mother and father bought

me a pair of overalls and I'd short pants underneath, so the boss said: 'You'd better take them off or they'll set on fire'.

So there I wer in mi short pants and sparks flying on mi legs, so I'd to try an get some moleskin trousers fer later. We always had a leather brat, but moleskins wouldn't fire the same. Another experience I had, we allus wore clogs and a piece of hot iron flew off down mi clog and I wer hoppin' round. I'd to put mi foot in't' water tub to cool it.'

Were there many cloggers in Bury when you were there?

'Yes, I remember quite a few. One on Rochdale Road called Matthews and Son. They did clogs and boots, and ther wer another one in George Street. Ther must have been eight or nine shops fer clogs then.'

Jean added that his sister bought Vincent a small pair of clogs for his Golden Wedding in memory of the days when he wore clogs. Vincent then showed me some cuttings from the *Bury Times* of his singing days. He got a record test with the *His Masters Voice* company, and after about three months they decided he could go and make some records with them; but his voice started to break, so they'd called it off.

Jean added, 'I wish mi grandson Ian had carried on in the trade. Wi begged and prayed of him to take it up, but no he didn't want to and he'd have bin med today if he had. Now he wished he had! Lady Towneley from Burnley had no one to shoe her horses and she came fer Vincent, and he's shoed horses fer her as well'.

I can just imagine you as the traditional blacksmith singing away at your work.

'Yes I did, and I did a lot of concerts too and once med over

£30 fer charity. £30 wer a lot of money them days. Just going back to the blacksmithing though, Mr. Ashcroft wer particular and every thing had to be just right. I'd to serve a seven-year apprenticeship and a went to nightschool at Newton Heath Technical School in mi clogs to learn about farriery. We had theory and practical and I'd to go fer an examination fer this certificate. One man who signed it wer Charles Richmond and he wer a big man in the Worshipful

Company of Farriers. Mi son Ralph had it framed and he wants it handed down fer future generations.

I must just tell you this story; it's a bit hard to believe in a way, but a went to St. Marie's school at Bury and wer friendly with a boy called Cornelius Carroll and thid 25 children. Thi used to have two sittings fer meals – one lot would eat first, then wash pots and cutlery, then lay the table fer the next lot. One man had to decorate the

bedroom, and he'd to step from bed to bed to do it; ther wer no room to move the beds. I can see ther father now, he wer an engine driver, and he had a big wax moustache and a silver watch on a chain. He wer a smart chap an all.

I've enjoyed mi life as a blacksmith I have.'

Vincent and Jean have just celebrated their Golden Wedding, and they have a marvellous family who are very proud of them.

Bill Waddington of Rossendale

'I was born in Holly Street, Bacup and I went to Cloughfold Council School. I had a good father and mother who saw that we went to Sunday School every week. Mi father and mother were good singers, in my opinion; and on Sunday evenings after tea they'd sit by the fire and sing hymns. Their voices blended well and this is perhaps why I developed an interest in music from an early age. I didn't play an instrument then, but I always went with the Irwell Brass Band. Mi cousin learnt to play the cornet, first with his father. Later he had professional tuition and did very well. In Bacup, at the Central School, we formed the first boys' brass band. There were thirty boys and it was started in 1915; I was a collector at the big houses in Bacup. Mi father used to take me to hear the band in Bacup a lot. We went on the tram and mi cousin, Clifford, played in the band. I learned to read music when I was 26, and the violinist who taught me later taught me to play the banjo. I was working as a barber and didn't have much time to practise so I gave it up! I wasn't

The Arcade, Waterfoot, in the early 1900s.

making progress anyway.

Mi father worked on the railway – first as a porter, then as a guard. There wer two railway stations in Bacup at that time. One was a private station which belonged to the Nadin family. The station was a 'Halt' on the way to Manchester so that the family could board the train on its way. They went to the 'Halt' by carriage and pair.

We wer living in Stacksteads, when I started work as a 'lather

boy' at the barber's shop and I wer eleven years old. When I wer thirteen, I went to work in the warehouse of a clog factory, tying clogs up. I later went as an apprentice to a barber in Waterfoot, where I stopped fer fifty years. In 'The Arcade' at Waterfoot only one business of a particular sort was allowed. There was an auctioneer; a doctors' surgery; a tennis shop; a gent's outfitters (Smith & Rawsons). On the other side, in

Burnley Road, was a greengrocer's; a milliner's; a chip shop; a jeweller's; a tailor's and a grocer's. Inside was a penny bank; an electrician; Schofield's; a florist's and a clock repairer. The arcade was built by Sir Henry Trickett. He was a machine manufacturer in Waterfoot and he later became a benefactor of our Bethel Chapel.

After serving five years as an apprentice barber, I became fully qualified. I learned the trade by first watching the barber then lathering. Then, after three years I started cutting hair. Later I wer allowed to shave customers, after practising on mi boss. We had private 'pots' in them days and each customer had his own shaving mug. We had one hundred private mugs, and lather brushes and all the mugs were numbered. When mi boss died, I took over the shop fer his wife fer two years until I was called up in the army. I wer certified Grade 4; unfit fer combat service. They told me to: 'put thi' clothes on lad before tha gets cowd'. I wer given a green card which meant I could be a fire watcher! Later on I became associated with Bethel Baptists Church, mi wife had always gone there. We had a choir and used to put on shows which ran fer ten weeks at a time. I learned to do electrical work as well, putting up the spotlights and floodlighting, etc. Then I became involved in painting the scenery. I got help from a local artist and made a good job of it. Afterwards, I joined the Rossendale Players as a stage hand. Bethel Baptists is on Burnley Road East. It was built by Sir Henry Trickett and it's a big church. As a Deacon of the church, I had to help organise the charity, set up by the benefactor, Sir Henry Trickett. New choir stalls were provided and I found the actual blueprint of that design when I was cleaning underneath the organ. The custom then, was fer a workman to leave some record of his work; and I've been given mementos over the years by people who knew of mi interest in them.'

Bill also collected matchboxes and told me:

'I had over twelve thousand at one time. I had a good friend in Northwich, Cheshire, who sent me stuff no-one else had. Mr Walter Meachel was his name.'

I learned to shave by practising on the boss and a balloon and he treated me like his own son. I retired at 66 and sold the business, but then it wasn't as busy though; fer shaves etc.

There wer three boys in mi family but there's only me left! I remember in Bacup, there was only the Liberal and the Conservative Party at first. Then they started the 'Workers Party'. Frank Howarth used to get a crowd around him on Irwell Street and later he became the Mayor of Bacup. In Waterfoot there was no Labour Party; but there was an I.L.P. and George Lupton was one. The Rev. Barton Turner was a Labour candidate in various parts of Lancashire (fer an M.P. that is). Captain Patrick was active in St. Ann's church fer some time as well.

I've always been a good reader and had an interest in history. I wrote an article about the 'Amazing Briton'. He was known on stage as a 'Strong Man'. He used to practise body-building in a barn. At that time there was an annual competition called 'Golden Fleece' which carried a prize and he won this prize! I traced his history through various records and followed his career fer a long time. He pulled a double-decker bus two hundred times with his teeth.

As a result of my contact with the 'Amazing Briton', I made contact with a Public Relations Officer of the Old Time Music Hall in Manchester and then London. I wrote essays fer them and provided them with cuttings about the theatre in Rossendale. Bacup Theatre wer made out of a foundry. Rawtenstall had a wonderful male voice choir and there is now the famous Rossendale Male Voice Choir.'

Bill knows a great deal more about the history of music and theatres in Rossendale, but I couldn't get it all down here. Suffice to say that the Rossendale Valley has a great tradition of choirs and singing. Bill is a very talented person and an asset to the Rossendale Valley. Unfortunately he has now lost his sight but that doesn't stop him from being interested in everything.

View of Waterfoot, looking towards Newchurch, taken in the 1950s. Bethel Chapel is the tall building with a steep roof in the centre of the skyline.

The Beautiful Rossendale Valley

The valley of Rossendale stands proud and firm
Surrounded by moorlands and hills,
From up at Loveclough down to Haslingden's line
Stand the chimneys of Rossendale's mills;
But the cotton mills now have gone into decline
And the shoe trade has taken their place –
It's away with the cloth caps and shuttles and looms,
Rossendale has now bred a new race!
Now there's lots to be seen in this Lancashire gem
It's become quite a tourist attraction,
For the modernised beauty of rivers and towns
Have provoked quite a startling reaction.
You can capture the splendour of Whitaker Park
Or the Lancashire tale of Waugh's Well.
Then there's old Irwell Vale or Bacup and Weir
And at Whitworth – tranquil Healey Dell.
See the beauty of Grane at sunrise or sunset
Or the history of Stubbylee Hall.
At Edenfield village gazing at the hills,
You'll rejoice in the moors most of all.
There's Rawtenstall Market and Newchurch and Lumb,
Up Edgeside; Whitwell Bottom or Weir.
There's no limit to what this fair valley contrives –
New attractions unfold every year.
Weaver's Cottage adds interest, reliving the times
Of clog-makers and the hand-weaving trade.
Whilst chapels and missions still uphold the truth
Of the Christian ideas that were made.
Yes, there's bigger and richer towns poorer by far
Than this staunch, gradely Lancashire vale
With its hills and its farms, its breath-taking charms
It's made EDEN on earth – ROSSENDALE.

Benita Moore

Margaret Creamer

'I was born in Brookside, Townsendfold, Rawtenstall and I went to Lea Bank Central school after I left the primary. It was the best school in the valley with a headmaster who believed in discipline; Mr. John Turner. He turned out some good scholars and all his staff were dedicated teachers.

My first job was wrapping toffee at Windle's toffee works, for ten shillings a week. My father's family were in business in a big way. However, even though there were fourteen members of the family left they never got the opportunity to take it over, so sadly, it went out of the family when my father died. We were always in haulage and transport though, and very well known for it in the Rossendale Valley. At one time we ran a taxi service to Moorlands for maternity cases! We also catered for wedding transport, group outings and funerals; we also had a big haulage branch of the business. My father was George Barnes and 'B' Barnes was the name of the company. We used to do an eight-day tour to Scotland for eight guineas (£38.40p).

The charabancs had solid tyres then. They were wagons all week but on a Friday night we had to change the bodies over to coaches. Each row of seats had a door at the side and we had all these to clean. The passengers took umbrellas because they had no protection from the elements. My dad was in the 1914/18 War at the time when horses provided pulling power. The drivers had to find their own way

Looking up Bacup Road from Queen's Square, Rawtenstall, in about 1910.
The mill visible on the right, along Bacup Road, is Ilex Mill

round the country as all the sign posts had been removed (this was in case German parachutists landed). We distributed meat all through the Valley, which was quite a job.

When my father died Alan Smith bought out the coach side of the company. I worked on the transport at the Town Hall for a number of years, then I came here to Ellen Smith's agency in Rawtenstall. I'm nearly seventy, but don't intend to give up work yet a while. When I was 21, in 1940, I, along with a lady in Glasgow, was the only woman with an H.G.V. Licence. I drove the coaches then, and I drove taxis on funerals. In those days there were no funeral parlours – bodies were just laid-out in coffins in their own front parlours, but that's all changed. All the town has become too impersonal in my opinion,

because everyone knew everyone else in those days. We have a lot of commuters now who travel to Manchester every day but have their homes in the Valley. The motorways are so handy for people.

Most of the old shops have gone – it's supermarkets now! I remember a shop which could fit out a lady from under garments to hat and gloves complete. There was a Boots chemist, two butchers etc., but the only shop left on the row is a Ladbrokes Betting shop. Rawtenstall market used to be open until nine o'clock on Saturday nights. We used to go at about 8.30 p.m. when fruit and vegetables were sold off. There was no refrigeration in those days, and wages were poor. My mother got eighteen shillings a week (80p) for cleaning the school, and that included looking after the boilers. My mother died at 45; she'd

always worked hard.

There were some real hovels round by the pub. There was also a rag and bone man. Friday was the day for cleaning windows and swilling the flags at the front door. There was more family life in the old days; we used to cut up old clothes to make pegged rugs on a piece of Hessian. Then there was the ritual of the tin bath. Modern people may have cleaner bodies but I don't think their minds are.

During the war my father's job included distributing petrol coupons to all the haulage contractors in Rossendale. Many good businesses have failed over the years; you've heard the saying: 'clogs to clogs in three generations', there's a lot of truth in that! Man and wife worked hard to build up a business and then paid for a good education for their children, but they took the back-bone out of the children in many cases, so the children spent what their parents had slaved for.

Rawtenstall has changed a lot but not always for the better. The churches are still well supported though. Traffic is the big problem, the roads just can't cope with it. Holiday fashions too have changed, people fly off abroad with less excitement than we got from a day in Blackpool.'

Margaret has been involved in haulage and transport all her life and is still working for the Ellen Smith Travel Agency in Rawtenstall. She's been with the firm for over ten years and always takes a great personal interest in people's tours and holidays whether just day trips or continental tours.

A lavishly-illustrated letterheading from Ilex Mill, Rawtenstall

Emma Edge of Waterfoot
aged 92 years

'I wer born at Dean Head Farm then we moved to Lower Barn Farm. I went to Heald School and then to work half time when I wer twelve at Broad Clough factory.'

What was your maiden name?

'Howorth, a real Rossendale name if ever there was! Living on a farm meant that we had plenty to do all of the time. When I was fifteen I went to learn weaving at Weir factory. This mill closed down so I went back to Clough factory on two looms. I know we'd to go to Sunday School; it didn't matter what sooart o' weather it wer, we'd to gooa. I got married when I wer 26. We'd to be'ave 'ussel' at Sunday School. We used to play in the fields an' many a time we 'ad a 'funeral'. We found a long piece of wood fer a coffin then we used to

reckon to bury these 'ere (whoever they wer, can't remember).

Mother wouldn't let us be noisy on a Sunday, we had to go Sunday School and Chapel. We used to have a field day and once we had a trip to Cleveleys. I joined the choir when I wer abeaut sixteen. We had 'trips' with the choir. I still remember the day when we sang: *Hail Smiling Morn*, as the coach was leaving. It wer lovely, really lovely and we wer home pretty early. You know, we allus had work to do on the farm when we got home from the mill, it wer hard work for mi mother as well as us.'

What entertainment was there?

'We had a Sunday School tea party and concert. I can still remember the first recitation I said; it wer called: *Little Boots and Shoes*.'

Can you remember how it goes?

'I am alone the lights burn low,
The sewing and mending done.
The little feet are all in bed,
Resting, everyone.
I'm weary as I go
My short night's rest to get,
But I'm weary with looking after
   the little ones.
Father's shoes stand at the end,
Guarding the little row.
Tired and weary are his feet
   . . .etc.
Sorry, I can't remember any more!

We had cattle on the farm and mi father went to Bacup to deliver milk every day.'

Did you have bad winters?

'Oh, they wer terrors! We often had to walk along the snow drifts to get to work; but we'd better

Mrs. Emma Edge has had a long and varied life,
and is well-known for the interesting talks she gives to women's groups.

summers than we have now. We went to Morecambe fer a week one holiday time and it wer terrible weather. When we got back mi father 'ad some hay ready fer geddin' in so we'd to pull us what-d'ya-call-its off – us best clothes – and put on us weekday clothes and start hay makin' 'till bedtime – mind you – bed time! I thought; What a home coming!'

Can you remember the market?

'Yes we had the market on a Wednesday in Bacup. We couldn't go very often because we wer workin'. We used to go to t' pictures on a Saturday night. We paid one penny to go in; another penny fer a vanilla and we had a halfpenny left fer some chips on the way home.'

Has Rossendale changed much over the years?

'Well, I come here to Waterfoot when I wer wed, and I've bin 'ere ever sin' and that's 62 years sin' next February. I've never moved, I fancy next move'll be in a box. I had one child but it didn't live.'

You're very well known for giving talks to women's groups, aren't you?

'Oh yes I am. Talks from the bible. I read my bible every day, it's on theer now. It gives me comfort on' there's nobody living whose more content than me; nobody, and I'm never lonely!'

How's that?

'I don't know, but I allus put mi trust in God. I've bin a widow fer twelve years; we had our Golden Wedding the year before.'

What about the women's organisations you speak to, are there a lot in the valley?

'Yes on' there's not many I've missed! Church of England I may not have been to much but all the Chapels in the valley I 'ave.'

What was it like when you first came to live here?

'Well there wasn't as much hooliganism as there is today. The Chapel I went to wer a really good one fer giving you some Christian background.'

Did you have electricity laid on?

'No we had no electric lights, nor gas. We had oil lamps and a coal fire. All the cooking wer done in the fire oven or on the fire. We did have running water though! I remember one very dry summer when we had to carry water. We had to have a lot of water fer the cattle; that wer a hard time!

We didn't go out much fer our entertainment but we had a gramophone at home, and we could allus tek us pals 'ome. I met a woman recently who used to come to our sing-songs. They could hear us in th' road. We used to belt id out thad loud. We 'ad a real good do. They can't mek their own entertainment th' same today.

When I'd been married a while I started to go to Hareholme Chapel an' I stopped there fer fifty years. I wer a superintendant there fer most of the time and I wer also secretary of the Ladies' Aid.'

Has a Chapel upbringing helped you in your life?

'Oh yes, because if you trust God you don't need to worry about owt else. I've a lot to thank God for. I do most of mi own housework and I do mi own washing. You can see I've an old-time rack on. I wouldn't part with that fer anything! I know people who did away with the drying rack and now wish they had them back.'

Do you still give talks to Ladies' Groups?

'Yes, I have three booked fer the next few weeks. I've been to one chapel every year a talking. I've no worries. Folks today are never satisfied. Mi mother med all her own bread until wartime when flour wasn't reliable. I never remember her buying cake.'

Have you any funny stories from your weaving days?

'Well we had lots of fun. I used to work wi a woman and do you know oo [she] come one day; I bet it wer ten years after! I didn't know her! I used to keep poultry and I wer comin' down th' road one day carrying two buckets of eggs and Fred (mi husband) wer stood at th' door. He says: 'There's sombri waiting fer thee in th' eawse.'

So when I come in I looks at this 'ere woman on' I couldn't remember at first who she wer, then it came to me who she wer! She came to work at Rawtenstall Mill and oo'd only bin working about a month when 'oo asked mi to save up for 'er.

I says: 'Save up for ya, ya don't know mi so well.'

Oo says: 'I know you're honest.'

So I saved up fer 'er and 'er an' 'er husband went away fer five days to Blackpool. I booked deawn every week wot she give mi; I think it come to abeaut five peaund at th'end. H'afe a creaun a week, or wer it five bob a week she give mi? When I give her this money at holiday time oo wer thrilled to bits. I did same year after an' thi went to Isle o' Man fer a week.'

Where were you when you kept poultry?

'We wer 'ere in Waterfoot. We had a hen pen. It wer tiring but I enjoyed doin' it.'

Any funny stories connected with the poultry?

'I daren't tell ya! Well go on then. One day th' parson wer gonna come to 'is tay [tea]. He wer coming at th' Tuesday, an' Fred 'ad gone eaut someweear. Well,

St. Mary's Parish Church, Rawtenstall, about 1920.

Fred used to pluck 'em, the chickens, an' I used to clean 'em. So this 'ere day I thought: 'Right, I'll kill this misell,' an' I wer trying to screw its neck but I mus'n't have done it properly 'cause when I put it deaun on th' flooar it got up and run away! I think I wer terrified of doin' it really.'

Did you have any concerts at chapel?

'Oh yes, and we went to other chapels as well: I allus took the tomfoolery part. I used to take mi book of lines to work and I wer allus talking to misell. I'll bet folk thought I wer goin' a bit queer. I learnt neerly all mi parts at work like that.'

Weaving would become monotonous day after day, wouldn't it?

'No not really. I liked it. I wer quite content with it. I wer married on the Saturday and worked a week up at Bacup, then I got four looms at Rawtenstall. There's more to weaving than some people realise. You can be a weyver fer fifty years and still learn.

I don't get up to Bacup very often now but I have some good friends who take me to the library at Rawtenstall. I'm real Lancashire, though. I used to talk broader 'ner I do neau. I wer talking to a woman up Lumb about gooin' away to Wales to a Christian Endeavour Home. She said: 'Will they be able to understand you?' But I managed! We had a lot of holidays at these Christian Endeavour Homes.'

Emma is a wonderful person, very kind and always good living. She still goes out giving her Christian talks and reads her bible every day. If everyone were like her the world would be a better place.

Frank Whittaker
of Waterfoot

I'd like to introduce Frank Whittaker who has a well known fruit and vegetable shop in Waterfoot. He's been in the trade for 43 years. He's also famous as a market trader in Bacup and Rawtenstall etc.

Anywhere else, Frank?

'Well, when I started it was in Waterfoot, at the market, but that's gone now.'

Right, we'll start there. Where were you born?

'In Rawtenstall at Ashgrove.'

When you left school, what work did you do?

'Well, I went into the Slipperworks, 'til I joined the army in 1942. I started off with the British Army then got attached to the American Army. We also supported the Foreign Legion and ended up with the Russian Army as well.'

Well, how did you manage all that, what regiment were you in?

'The Royal Field Artillery, which worked very hard.'

You certainly got moved around a lot then, I bet it was quite an experience. Have you anything to say about that time; any incidents that come to mind?

'Yes. I was actually a prisoner of war and the action was at Sionaza

in North Africa. It was the 155th field battery and over three weeks we had to hold out a line within 25 miles of our own lines and we finished up with nineteen men. I've been told since that the battery was awarded the V.C. but I've never tried to find out if that wer true. I would have to write to records to find out, but I've never bothered; it's all water under the bridge now.'

So what happened when you were demobbed, that would be around 1946. Did you come back to Waterfoot?

'Oh yes, I did and I got married and we lived in Waterfoot. Then it was pulled down and we've lived in Hardman Drive ever since.'

What made you go into the fruit and vegetable trade?

'Well, I was only eighteen when I joined the army and there was nothing else really when I came back.'

Waterfoot would be fairly quiet, then?

'Well, I couldn't go back to the job I was doing at eighteen. What sort of job would that be when I was married?'

You'd been a slipperworker, hadn't you?

'Yes, for about four years.'

I don't suppose you got a good wage then?

'No. When I started I got 4/6d a week for 48 hours which isn't so much.'

Tell me about the shop you started in Waterfoot. Was there a market in Waterfoot then?

'Yes there was, just over the road from Mullard's. In fact, Mullard's took it over after it had closed down.'

And did your shop make a do in those days?

'Before the war, Waterfoot had the best market for miles around. The reason it closed was the Corporation. They wouldn't black it out during the war, so people coming home at half past five from the factories found everybody gone, because it was dark at half past four. They couldn't light up, so

that's why it went!'

I suppose people came from Bacup, as well?

'Oh yes; they came from Newchurch; Cowpe; Waterfoot and Hareholme. It was a fantastic market was Waterfoot.'

What days was it on?

'Oh, only on a Friday.'

Right, so you had your shop opposite to where the market used to be. I know it's hard work, my sister had a vegetable shop and you've to be up early morning to go and get your fruit etc. You've done this 43 years, then?

'That's right, I still am; doing it that is!'

You've also stood the market in other places. Where did you go?

'Where? For buying goods and stock?'

No, where you had stalls for yourself, I mean.

'Oh, I'd one in Rawtenstall and one in Bacup and one here and the shop as well.'

And have you been doing those for forty-odd years as well?

'Oh yes, everyone of them.'

Well how have shopping habits changed?

'Well in those days there weren't any fridges, I mean today people buy meat and put it in a deep freeze. In them days you bought it

WATERFOOT -1891-

The photographer is obviously an object of interest to the flat-capped and bowler-hatted men and boys outside Waterfoot's 'New Market' in 1891.

daily or no more than two days at once; you couldn't keep it fresh, you see.'

I suspect that Waterfoot is still a traditional area where you'll get your regulars coming in every week?

'The problem is, again, you get all this here one-stop shopping like a supermarket thing. It doesn't mean you're probably any better off, but for some people it's simpler to do that, plus the fact they don't need cash – they can produce a plastic card which never used to be! It was always money over the counter and everybody knew where they were. They'll go and buy this, that and the other, get 10p off cigarettes even if they don't need two hundred, just to save 10p, then they go and pay with their Barclaycard and wait a fortnight to get their bill.'

'Course you're quite right; things these days are easier. There's no ways of thrift these days. Do you know anything about Waterfoot? What's this name 'Baltic' I've seen – Baltic Bridge, Baltic House, Baltic Mill etc.?

'Well, they're named for the factory there; they made felt.'

Was that the name of the firm?

'Well, they had two or three firms – four I think. I can't remember all their names. Now across the road opposite the mill there used to be a big house, and the last person to live in it was Dr. Anderson. It's now a car park and where you go in there used to be some massive big gates and there were all poplar trees and gardens. Next to the big house there was a coach house for the coaches and horses to go in.'

For him? The doctor I mean.

'Oh yes and for the big house; and for those that had it previous to him. They had these big, fancy wrought iron gates, about eight feet high.'

I suppose Waterfoot would come under Rawtenstall then, would it?

'Yes, Rawtenstall Council, but these were the original shops built in 1840. I don't remember, but my mother lived here and my father was a police sergeant in Waterfoot. Each shop down this line had a little garden to it then.'

This is Bacup Road, isn't it?

'Yes and the garden was only small, about six feet and you went thro' a gate to get to the shop. This place was originally the ale-house when it was built.' (Frank indicates the back of the shop.)

Kathleen Whittaker, Frank's wife calls out 'Don't forget to put St. James' Church on the map!'

Kathleen has just mentioned the Church, St. James', which is the Parish Church. Go on, tell me a bit about it.

'It's over a hundred years old but we have dry rot and we need £50,000 pounds.'

Frank's wife now joins in the conversations.

Frank was just telling me that this used to be the ale-house.

'Yes it was and folks didn't sit down around like they do now – they used to bring a jug! They'd put the barrel on what they used to call a stillage and they'd pour it out into the jug and they'd go back home. They didn't sit in as you can see from the size of the building; they couldn't, they just filled their jugs and took it home.'

Was there not a bench where the old men would sit and swop stories?

'Well they might o' done but there wasn't much room. Mind you there weren't so many people then.'

Why? Was it a small population?

'Yes, there were no estates or anything like that. There was just like Newchurch; Cowpe and Waterfoot; the older parts.'

What about the people from up the Valley, you know like Burnley Road East? It fascinates me because it's a long road and there's only little buildings and little shops; very parochial!

Frank speaks again now: 'That's why it's built like that; it's what we call 'rhythm' building. Because it's in a valley you can't build very well up the sides and so forth, up Cowpe Road etc.'

What about the mills?

'Well there's none left – hardly.'

Were they all slipperworks, or what?

'No, one was a pickle shop and t'other was a felt place. One was Greenbridge Slipper Factory and the other one I think, burned down. I think it was rubber or something. It was on the left of Cowpe Road, on the bend. I remember that being on fire 'cos my dad took me up. I was only about three or four years old. I can just about remember that, but most of the mills have gone now.'

And yet there's a long winding road up the Valley, isn't there, where the mills were?

'There were quite a lot of factories up there in the '20s and '30s. It was the 'Golden Valley' then, was this. People would come from

Bury, Accrington and Rochdale to work here. You see, they have the rivers on every valley, for power.'

I see, cheap power, wasn't it?

'That's it! They had a big water wheel at Cowpe, a massive one, and they pulled that down in about 1949 or something like that.'

Coming here now, I've been surprised at Waterfoot – there's all these shops and there's Dick Ireland with his little industry at the back.

'They've just pulled the railway bridge down now.'

That's over Cowpe Road, isn't it, up to the village?

'Yes, it's all gone now, the bridge I mean.'

What about all these little arcade shops here?

'That arcade was built by Sir Henry Trickett. You went inside the arcade, but you don't do now. There were shops inside there, a billiard hall; shops of everything then.'

Now you've stood Bacup Market for 43 years. How have you gone on in the bad winters after the war?

'Well, we just had to stand it, that wer all.'

You never got blocked in, in the glen, or anything, did you?

'Oh we've had to leave the vehicle down here, many a time, when you couldn't get over because of the snow. My father stood in 1907 at Bacup Market.'

Did he really! What was he called?

'Giles Whittaker. They didn't have

electric light in those days. They had what they call carbide lights. You know, you used to put water and some carbide and then there were gas in and if the wind blew too hard, it blew them out, and they'd have to light them again.'

Was he fruit and vegetables as well?

'Oh no! They had homemade sweets and soap. The market used to be on 'til 9 or 10 o'clock at night. I'm not sure which. We were coming home one day, there was a blizzard and I said to my father, 'How did you go on, Dad, this weather?' They didn't have vehicles, you know; they had hand carts then, and they walked it from Rawtenstall all up here to Bacup market. They'd start about lunchtime – not 8 o'clock in the morning, like now, but they went on 'till late at night. He said, allus they would do in a blizzard was keep going and hope they didn't get their wheels stuck in the tram lines.'

I'll bet he lived to be a good age, too.

'He was 74 when he died.'

So, were there trams going up the valley then?

'Oh, yes.'

Where did they go to, Bacup?

'They went to Bacup and there were trams into Rochdale and they'd trams up this road here to Waterfoot. They didn't go any further than that. My grandfather was a police sergeant in Waterfoot about 1902 'til 1910.'

So he would be the proverbial 'village bobby' then. I bet he'd have some tales to tell, wouldn't he? Can you remember any particular old characters round the markets at Waterfoot?

An open-topped motor 'bus chugs up Burnley Road, Crawshawbooth, just before the First World War.

'Well, there was always someone hanging around and there was one on Bacup market, they called him 'Robert the Devil', that's what we used to call him. He was round the market all the time. He'd sweep up and he was always cadging cigarettes. Now we had a market inspector called Billy Laycock at that time and Robert would go to him in the morning because he hadn't a regular job. Billy would give him 6d and tell him to go and have a shave. He gave him 6d every Wednesday and every Saturday to go and get shaved before he went on the market. Then they had a market trip to Blackpool and they said: 'We'll take Robert with us'. He'd never been to Blackpool in his life, and he was seventy-odd. So they sat him on the front seat of the coach and gave him a packet of Woodbines and told him that they would find him some more when he had finished them. He got himself ready, all dressed up (he always had clogs on) and they took him to Blackpool and it was the first time he had ever seen the sea. They went in a hotel and sat him at the top of the table to have his tea.

I remember another thing; it was Good Friday morning and we were cutting fish up and I could hear these clogs coming down. Anyway, Robert came through the door and we said: 'Wher' t' going Robert?' He said: 'I'm going to Cowburn's.' (This was another greengrocers up Haslingden.) Time went on and it got toward 12 o'clock, so Robert comes past and he's carrying one of those four-gate-legged tables on top of his head. So we said: 'Where are you going?' He said: 'I'm going up to Bacup.' So we said: 'All right.' Anyway we finished off half an hour after, so we went off up toward Bacup through the glen; and there's Robert sat on this table in the middle of the glen. There were a lot of characters then but today they don't bother. If you were in trouble in them days they'd come and help you straight away, you didn't need to ask.'

There wouldn't be as much need for hospital treatment and such, would there?

'I know during the depression, they would bring children in and make a big potato pie, so they would all have something to eat; they all got their share.'

Do you remember Jack Crawshaw, he was a cobbler, I think?

'Oh yes, he lived up Cowpe. He lives opposite Cowpe School. Going back to the 1920's there was a clogger at Scout Bottom. I think he was called Carey Hargreaves and then Jim Davidson had a shop. He, the clogger, were called Nuttall at Rawtenstall, and then there was Crawshaw's and there was another shop at Stacksteads, a clogshop, I can't remember any more.'

Is there anything else about Waterfoot, anything you think should be mentioned. Obviously you've been here forty-odd years.

'Well, I've been here 66 years, actually. They've pulled all the best places down – Newchurch; Bridleway; this is what they want for the tourists and they've pulled it down. Places built 350 years ago have gone, you can't replace it once it's pulled down.'

Have you anyone to follow you in the business?

'No, my daughter's a sister at Manchester Royal. Besides, it's not a woman's job, really.'

Your wife mentioned St. James' Church. Are there any more little churches. There's Woodlea Mission, isn't there?

'Yes, there was Woodlea Mission and there was one higher up – the Scout's School. There's the Methodist at Hareholme; St. James' in Waterfoot; Bethesda – they pulled that one down. There's a Methodist just up the road and, further up there's Wesleyan's at one side and another at the other side of the road. Then there's St. Peter's Roman Catholic, then the Newchurch Church and Bethlehem too.'

It looks like religion played a big part in the valley. You've still got the Baptist Ladies – the older end would remember them mostly, I suppose?

'Oh yes, there wasn't much to do in those days and my dad said that if we didn't go to Sunday School we couldn't be in the cricket team! But of course the big mill owners, they used to put the money into it. They'd have their bring and buy sales. The woollen factory would send about ten blankets up. Cotton factory sent about twenty pairs of

sheets – stuff like that, you see. This was how the churches kept going, they put the money into it.'

It was a good thing because they were their workers, and they looked after them, then. The employment now apart from the shoe industry, is gone so they'll have to go out of the valley. Most of the young people do, don't they?

'Yes, there's nothing here for them at all. The main factories have gone.'

Tell me about your aunts.

'Well, I used to have some old aunts. They lived to be about 96 or 99 and they were all spinsters and I used to like talking to them as they could tell me a lot. They used to come here and one of them called 'Aunt Bessie' was a suffragette and tied herself to the railings in London!'

Was she there with Mrs Pankhurst? Was she a Whittaker?

'No she was called Bryce. There were three of them but they never lived together, they were always falling out. But they were very interesting to listen to and they had very good memories and they could tell you what had gone on. When I buried my Aunt Minnie, I opened the grave – and that grave hadn't been opened since the 1800s. There were only six graves then, because it was a new cemetery. It must have been sixty years before, since it were opened; her brother had died pretty young and she was the only other one in.'

Now the other one – the suffragette – that was pretty unusual for someone round these parts, wasn't it? After all Waterfoot is only a small place, compared with, say, Manchester, with its larger population?

'Oh yes, but Aunt Bessie was politically minded and though she was a spinster she knew what she was talking about. Yes, she was with Mrs Pankhurst's ladies. Probably when you've gone, I'll remember lots of other things.'

It was very interesting talking to Frank. He's retired now, but still works hard, and his wife Kathleen helps raise money for the church.

The 'Glen' is a lovely wooded part of the road between Waterfoot and Stacksteads. *You can see part of the old railway line up to Bacup by the side of the road.*

Richard Ireland

Black pudding maker

'I was born in Barnoldswick and mi mother died when I wer five years old, so I then came to live in Edenfield – with mi grandma. There was a big family of Irelands in Edenfield and mi father worked fer Dr. Ford. When I left school I went butchering. First I went to Peel Brow school in Ramsbottom, then I worked at Kay's Butchers in Edenfield, near the Coach & Horses Inn. I later joined the navy and after the war returned to butchering at the Haslingden C.W.S. – I was about 21 then.

I'd made black puddings when I worked in Edenfield, but only in a small way. A man called Harold Elton taught me how to make them, but as the war was on, the ingredients were hard to get hold of. I seemed to be the only person working at the Co-op who was able to make black puddings, so I started making them again. I also supplied Taylor's butchers on Blackburn Road, Haslingden. Later, I bought a shop of mi own at Stubbins in 1952 and I made puddings on and off down there

Then there wer two factory fires in Stubbins, both on the same night! It wer just like the blitz! The whole village wer evacuated and the people wer housed in school rooms. We jumped in the car and went up the top road, near the farm. Suddenly, Gladys (mi wife) said: 'Where's the money, all the shop takings?' I didn't know, so I left Gladys at the farm and went back down to the village. Fire tenders and hoses wer all over the place, but I managed to get to mi shop. It seemed there was a fear that the factory chimney would fall, but in the event it didn't. The four storey building just folded in like a pack of cards. When I went to bed on the night of the fire I had a good business, the next morning I had nothing. All mi customers who worked at the mill lost ther jobs so thi couldn't come to the shop.

I started working in Waterfoot where I continued to make black puddings. I then worked fer another butcher fer a while, then got mi own shop again. I still made the puddings fer two or three other butchers and they were very popular. I had the shop fer about ten years, then I had a 'bad do' with shingles. I still carried on with the business though until a man came along who made me a good offer for it, so I sold it to him.

I then took the first holiday I'd ever had in mi life – a week in Cornwall. Then it was suggested that I make a commercial job of this black pudding making, so I did. It just snowballed and snowballed. The first week I made 250 lbs of black puddings. I used to make them in the little place out back, but now I work in the former slaughter house.'

Dick Ireland with a fine display of his 'special recipe' black puddings.

Did you make them to your own special recipe, which you don't divulge?

'Yes. I can tell you some of the ingredients. Basically, blood; fat; onions; barley; oat meal; sausage rusks; flour and seasoning. Twelve different sorts of seasoning including salt and pepper.'

What are skins made of?

'Intestines – ox intestines which, of course, had to be well cleaned. The dry ingredients are all mixed well together. The pork fat which has been cut up is then cooked along with the onions which are minced. All these are sieved then mixed together. There's no rind on the pork it's just pure back fat. The mixture is then ready for the filler which is done by hand. As I said, the first week I made 250 lbs – now I make 2,000 lbs! I've a good market in Manchester for mi puddings. I delivered 700 lbs there this morning, and I supply twelve shops and market tenants in Bury. I supply a wholesaler in Manchester whose customers come from as far as Cheshire and North Wales, amongst others. Mi nephew is a meat inspector for one of the councils. I also have a girl who works in the business.'

It seems you could do with more staff you're so busy?

'Well yes; as a matter of fact I've been today to see about another building. If I can get a bigger building I'll train someone to work full time.

We (Rossendale) have a twin town in Germany and I was informed by Haslingden Council that German television would like to do a documentary featuring me making black puddings. I said they wer welcome to come providing they wer prepared fer a very dirty job (some people can't stand it). Anyway, they sent someone over and when he landed he said: 'I

won't keep you more than twenty minutes' (this was about 11.30 am). He left at 12.50 pm. A couple of weeks later I got a 'phone call from Germany, from Cologne. It was this man Joseph and I was invited to Germany to appear on this TV programme called: 'Hello Friends'. I was invited to just enjoy miself so I went! I just had to demonstrate making black puddings on film. I took all the ingredients with mi, along with 40lbs of puddings. I also make the German sausages which are sliced and fried. A lot of these go to Birmingham and also to the North Country Foods firm, which has a depot in Garstang. I have customers from Blackpool and Fleetwood, and I have a regular customer in Bangor, Northern Wales.'

I'm surprised you have a woman working amongst blood and all the rest of it.

'Oh it doesn't bother Sally at all! She won't mix the puddings but she washes all the utensils, that doesn't bother her. I started the black pudding business just as something to do, but its just grown and grown. They're more in demand away from here though, they get a good price for them! There's one fellow lives in the bottom house here who went to a place in Cheshire. He got a black pudding cut in the shape of a star, he paid £1.75 fer it. It was in a big hotel in Cheshire. Black puddings used to be a poor man's meal but now they are a gourmet dish. I supply many of the big hotels in Manchester, I recently had an order for about 150 small puddings and this was for a special function at the Piccadilly Hotel in Manchester.'

How do you get them in the skins?

'Well, you just fix the intestine on a tube on the end of the machine. The filling is pushed by the

machine into the tube and through into the skin, it then forms a long sausage. String is tied round and the puddings are knotted up into bunches. I get the blood from Great Harwood, it's ox blood, I use a hundred gallons a week. I still weigh everything, I insist on this because guess work doesn't do! If everything is weighed you get the same product every time. I make a frying pudding as well. This is made in a block and can be put in a pie, er sliced and fried. I really have as much work as I can cope with until I get a bigger place. I'll know in the morning if I've got this place er not.

I remember one time when I was working at Haslingden, the boss came in at 5 o'clock, and we finished at 5.30 pm. I had to catch a bus to Edenfield at 5.35, to get home to Stubbins. The boss ordered me to go to Accrington to collect two 'Kits', i.e. metal cans of blood. I says: 'It's five o'clock.'

'I've told you,' he said 'two kits of blood from Accrington.'

Well I got into the van and collected the blood. On mi way back I had to brake hard to avoid children in the road. I heard an ominous bump in the back of the van. The blood container had fallen over and the blood wer pouring out of the back door of the van, like a waterfall! Just imagine, twenty gallons of blood all over the road. I had to run the van into the yard and put the hose pipe on it to get rid of all that blood! We had to ring up the slaughter house early the next morning to have more blood delivered so we could start work. I heard later that the police were called to investigate the source of all this blood which was running all over the road because of traffic driving through it. I said nowt so I heard no more about it.'

Dick is a marvellous man, who still enjoys his work, and his reputation continues to grow every year because of his delicious 'Black Puddings'.

Arthur Crabtree

Grocer at Stacksteads for over 50 years

Arthur Crabtree behind the counter of his well-stocked family grocer's shop

Tell me about your shop, Arthur.

'Well, we still weigh rice up here in my shop; it's not ready packed like in the supermarkets.'

Tell us a bit about your early days then.

'I was born in Primrose Street in Stacksteads and I went to the Council School then to the Grammar School (Bacup and Rawtenstall Grammar School, that is).'

What did you want to do when you left school?

'Well we just did what we had to do in them days! I left school at sixteen and came to work in this shop. It belonged to my uncle, James Crabtree and we worked from 7am to 9pm. Everything came in bulk then and had to be weighed up. Grain was stored in bins and was also weighed up as required for all the customers. Butter was stored in casks down in the cold cellar. The butter was actually Danish, but because it was shipped from Kiel in Germany it was known as 'Kiel' butter. If Danish butter was more than ten days old we could send it back. These are the pats for shaping the butter (Arthur held up 2 wooden pats). We always put some water with the butter to help to shape it. We hadn't much competition in those days and we used to go out for orders on a Monday and deliver by horse and cart on the Tuesday. There were no supermarkets, and travellers used to call for orders from our stocks. One traveller always used to call at 5.30pm on a Wednesday. We ordered confectionery from 'Lyons' in London and these goods were delivered here at 12.00 noon on a Friday. They'd never get here now because we've lost the railway; this was how our goods were transported. The porter brought them from the station on a cart. Our customers used to come in with carpet bags; they bought flour and barm (yeast), all the people were nice. The market was at Bacup and stalls were still there at 9.00pm in the gaslight.'

Did you have bad winters?

'Well they weren't right good. There was a snow plough attached to a steam tram to clear the lines sometimes.'

Any amusing incidents you remember?

'Well, one chap used to come; he lived at Rawtenstall, near the market. He had a grocers shop and used to make lemon cheeses. His one 'chip on the shoulder' was providing a free bag for five pounds of potatoes. He sold the grocers and took the 'selling out' shop next door (off licence). His customers were the same people who'd come to his grocer's shop, but they wouldn't pay a penny for a potato bag. They'd buy him a pint but refused to pay for a bag. One chap had a grocer's next door to a greengrocer's and a woman came every morning for ten pounds of potatoes. She never brought a bag and he got fed up with this so he opened the bottom of the bag and gave it into her arms full of potatoes. When she got outside the potatoes fell through the bag onto the floor; she always brought a bag after that! People don't eat like what they used to though. Children go to school without a drink; they buy a tin of 'pop' and a packet of crisps for their breakfast. Not a bit of good in that! We had bacon and eggs every morning. I remember calling for a friend on the way to school and the frying pan was on the middle of the table; the children were dipping their bread in it and I could have eaten some more.'

'I'm the only *family* grocer from Bacup down to Rawtenstall; the others are 'shop keepers'. All the stuff sold now is rubbish compared with what we used to sell. If you bought a tin of 'Del Monte' pears, say about Christmas time, you were really getting Californian; it all depends on the season. We then got fruit from Greece and Australia and now we get rubbish from . . . I won't say where! We have the old 'Indian Brandee' here; it's a very old fashioned remedy. A young lady came in for some this morning. Now whether she's going to a bottle party or not I don't know. It's really the older people that buy that kind of old fashioned product though; the young ones go to the doctor, they don't believe in all that sort of thing. We always have time to chat with our customers later and find out if these remedies work.'

Were there many big families then?

'Yes most people had big families round here. There were quarries at the back and the men were 'frozen out' in the winter so they couldn't pay their bills; so they paid when they could. But everybody knew everyone and trusted them. They used to say: 'If you kicked one, they all limped.'

They used to make broth in an iron pan which simmered on the fire and it lasted all week and improved in flavour every day. People buy all the pre-packed food now – they can't be bothered to cook a 'proper' meal.'

When will you retire?

'Oh, they die when they retire up here!'

I could talk forever about this old fashioned shop – like something from the past. The atmosphere is incredible; it's been going for about one hundred years. The same wooden counter, and bacon machine; butter pats; Indian Brandee and carbolic soap. Old bottles of sauce; nothing seems to have changed and Mr Crabtree seems quite happy to stay another ten years. Such wonderful dedication to his work and loyalty to his customers over the past 55 years has ensured that Arthur Crabtree still has a valued place in the local community and in everyone's hearts. He truly is the friendly, personal, typical 'FAMILY GROCER'.

Thomas Bolton's grocer's shop (prop. T. Duckett) in the 1920s.

Thowd Corner Shop

Ah like t' let mi memory stray
To th' corner shop deawn eawr way,
It wur nobbut jest at th' end o' th' street
An noan so far to trail thi feet

It wer allus noan as 'thirty four'
Wi a big brass knocker on th' door,
An on Saturday tha cud spend thi penny.
Me an eawr Joe, an little Jennie.

Mi Mam ud hev a shippin list
Salt; fleawr; an jam; an eawnce o' twist,
Twist fer mi Dad; he had a pen,
He used t' warm i' th' coil pit then.

Th' Shop Keeper's name wur: 'Mrs. Briggs',
Her husband smooked them fancy cigs,
Ah think th' called em 'Craven A'
They wer nobbut a tanner anyway.

By gum the things hoo used t' sell –
Brushes an buckets, toycars as well;
Sealin' wax an balls o' twine,
Nougat bars, a penny a time!

But neaw, Thowd Corner Shop's pulled deawn,
An thur's no such thing as haulf a creawn,
An' fags an' Condor's seventy p
An things er not what they used t' be.

They say as things ur better neaw
Wi th' Super Market everywhere,
They dasht' t' bingo all of a flutter
An some of em cornt tell Stork fro' Butter.

So ah like t' let mi memory
Job back t' th' shop as used t' be,
When me Mam ud sheawt: 'Thee fotch some butter
An keep thi new shoon eawt o' th' gutter'.

Tom Swift

George and Annie Ormerod

I've come to see George and Annie Ormerod of Bacup. They've lived in the same house for 50 years and they have an open fire which you don't see very often these days. George, amongst other things, used to work in the pit!

Where were you born and bred George?

'In Bacup; in George Street, but I've lived in the Greenend district nearly all mi life.'

And where is that district?

'Along this bottom where we live now [Edward Street].'

Which school did you go to in Bacup then?

'The Mount – up Lane End, at Bacup.'

And how old were you when you finished there?

'Well, when I finished at Mount, I went to what they called the Central School, but they changed the name to Thorn School later.'

What was your first job when you left school?

'Weaving – in the cotton; Joshua Hoyle's, Beech Mill, half-time. I stuck it there 'til 1923 and then I went in the pit.'

Didn't you like weaving – is that why you left?

'Well, I wanted to be amongst fellows you see.'

Which pit did you go to then?

'Top Pit – it's on the moors between Stacksteads and the village of Water. I had about two miles over the moors to walk. Ther wer no transport.'

How did you go on in the snow?

'Well, you had it to do; no walls to shelter at th' back of. We used to empty t' water out of us clogs when it wer raining.'

Could you get dry when you got to the pit or had you not to bother?

'Well we used to leave things to dry as best we could. We had it to walk there and back every day.'

And what did you say about not paying you for travelling time if it were snowing or raining?

'No, they didn't then; but when thi got nationalised – if buses couldn't run, we had to wait an hour in a morning fer a bus; and if the bus didn't come in that hour, we could go home and get paid fer it.'

I see, like waiting time; and what were the conditions like down the pits in the 1920s?

'Oh they were rough! Then th' pit where I worked – the coal wer only sixteen er eighteen inches high.'

How did you manage that?

'You had to keep ripping part of the roof down so we could get in. It wer hard work wer that. It wer near the roof, and the nearer the

George Ormerod – a man who has acquired many skills during his life.

roof the thinner the coal seam. The deeper you go, the thicker the coal seam. We had to buy our own candles in a packet; they had a number on but I can't remember what it wer now.'

Did you put them on your helmet?

'No, we had a lump o' clay and you moulded it round t' candle and stuck it on the back of the tub; you know – the wagon.'

Your wife was saying about a 'Scabby Back'.

'Yes, it wer so low that on Monday mornings you'd lie on yer stomach wi tears running down yer cheeks; you'd have knocked all the scabs off yer back.'

It's a wonder you didn't get infected, because there wouldn't be any Pit Baths then.

'No there weren't. We had to wait 'til we got home to have a bath.'

I suppose you'd a tin bath which you had to fill up. Were you in this house then?

'No in 1939 I was working at Templey's Sanitary Pipe Works going toward Todmorden at time when we come in here.'

What about your childhood days. What did you do for entertainment then?

'We played tig in t' ring and billet and stick, things like that.'

Did you go down t' market much at Bacup?

'No, not when we wer young, we'd no time er money.'

You were saying there were quite a few pits in Bacup.

'There were that many – thi couldn't sell the coal! In Todmorden Road there were Sharneyford Pit; one at Oakenclough Mill; Sandy Road Pit; one up Rochdale Road – what thi all called 'The Mucky Hole', because ther wer that much water in it – it wer slutchy. It wer just agen t' George and Dragon, not many yards from t' main road; where thi went under. Then up Burnley Road ther wer Tall

Meadows, Whittaker Clough and Deerplay.'

Of course there's none open now is there?

'No. Then ther wer Grimebridge; Foxhill – I can't remember them all, ther wer that many pits. They wer selling coal at 10 pence a hundredweight at Tall Meadows Pit and at Sharneyford and Stacksteads, and they'd lend you a truck to bring it home in as well.'

You have an open fire now. Is that smokeless? What does that cost you now for a hundredweight, about £4 or £5?

'It's more like £7-odd these days.'

A big difference to 10 pence! I suppose if the mines were all working today, coal would be cheaper than electricity or gas wouldn't it?

'Oh yes. You'd be surprised how the Rossendale Valley is undermined. All them pits – it wer 'wick' wi 'em. And most of them were George Hargreaves' Collieries.'

Your daughter-in-law told me you were famous for having a cart to do 'flittings' on.

'I've done hundreds of 'em! I had a four wheeled lorry as well.'

And what about these horses you had?

Oh I love horses. I'd rather have a horse and trap now than a car, because if you were going anywhere you could see all the scenery. You've passed in a flash in a car.'

What about the salerooms?

'Oh I used to do all the carrying there. Greenwoods' Salerooms, where 'Healds' is now. First pony I

had fer seven years and then I sold it. I don't know where it got to when I sold it. Then eighteen months later it come back. I tried to buy it back but they wouldn't part wi it. It belonged to Doctor Brooks up Water. He sent his chauffeur fer it; they still wouldn't sell it. Then I sold another to a farmer aside of the pub and that come back three days afterwards.'

I've heard of dogs doing that but not horses. So you must have treated them well.

'I started wi pigs round about same time – breeding 'em. We wer allowed to kill three full 'uns fer us own use during rationing, but we had to surrender our bacon coupons. Then they cut it to two. First pig I had, if I left gate open it would come up here into the backyard.'

Was it quite friendly? And what were the names of some of your horses?

'Yes she was. One of the horses wer called 'Billy'. Then ther was 'Bonnie'. I sent that to Bleakholt later. I bought that horse and I didn't want it. I bought it at an auction farm sale at Rawtenstall. I see a fellow keep bidding at this horse and I decided he wasn't getting it because he wer a horse slaughterer from Burnley. I had it a year er two and I wer going up that street at th' bottom there and ther wer a row of garages there. One silly devil backed out of his garage; nobody wer guiding him, and the horse got its front leg between the bumper and car and it went lame and it couldn't work so I sent it to Bleakholt.'

Have you carried any strange things in your cart?

'Yes. I've been there when couples were splitting up and been arguing about what they wer having and then th' police ud come and

sometimes the bailiffs. Sometimes I'd have to get stuff off th' cart and fly off out of the way. I have a photo wi loads o' kids on mi cart.'

Mind you, if you had a little lorry, you were getting on a bit from the horse and cart weren't you?

'Well you'd a heck of a job to get a licence then at that time fer a motor, with the War being on. Ther wer three licences then called A, B and C, and there was one licence where you were only allowed to travel 25 miles with it and you could go practically anywhere; and I forget what the other was. I've still got mi licence fer the horse and cart though.'

How long were you in the pit?

'I wer in the pit about forty years.'

You've seen a lot of changes then. Which pit were you at when you left?

'Deerplay – going toward Burnley then right again th' Deerplay pub.'

What do you remember about the market?

If you'd paid yer way and you'd ten bob left you wer laughing. A rabbit; a cabbage; 5lb potatoes; 1lb onions; 1lb carrots all fer one shilling and if you went on the market on Saturday night; as much beef as you could carry fer 2/6d (half-a-crown).'

Of course then there were no fridges or freezers so they had to 'get rid' hadn't they? And did the trams used to come from Rawtenstall then?

'Yes they used to come up to the Market Hotel from Rawtenstall, but Rochdale trams came round by the centre near the King George.'

But I think a lot of people who

were born in Bacup have remained in Bacup haven't they?

'I wouldn't like to live anywhere else; not in the valley.'

It's about thirteen or fourteen miles from Accrington and I've said to people: 'Do you ever get to Accrington?' and they say: 'No.' Of course now the buses run right through Bacup to Accrington. Anything else you'd like to talk about?

'Well, I don't think you see life working in the pit like anybody else, because you're underground most of the time and if you were on shift work it wer worse still. I've seen me if we've been on afternoons – I've nearly slept too long to catch th' bus on the

afternoon shift because I was up in the morning. I'd have mi dinner, sit against a good fire and doze off.'

It would seem all bed and work wouldn't it, because you'd eight hours on and you'd come home to eight hours sleep so it would only leave about two hours fer entertainment?

'Same as in wintertime. It wer dark when you went to the pit and it wer dark when you got home. We only had weekends that's all.'

And how about the bad winters in 1947 etc?

'We had to walk on the walls up to Deerplay one morning and it got to The Roebuck did the bus that's all. We had a bit of a natter and when

th' bus didn't come, we walked on top of the walls from Roebuck to Deerplay to get to work. It wer 9 o'clock that morning when wi landed. Wi draws our wages week after an they'd knocked the time off fer being late and wi decided wi wouldn't do it again and wi didn't. Though we did get paid fer it after causing some bother.'

What about holidays. Did you go to Blackpool?

'Yes. Mostly Blackpool. It wer 7d return to Rochdale and we used to book to Wardle Station.'

Up to the 60s the trains were running up to Bacup. Diesel trains weren't they?

'I couldn't just say when them

Horse-drawn delivery carts, including a coal wagon, in Market Street, Bacup in 1900.

finished. I know at morning and after tea you could tell th' time wi 'em with th' whistle blowing. I used to blow th' whistle at Stacksteads Pit at 7.30 every morning. That wer when Farholme Mill wer going; you know, cotton, and Baxters Brewery at 'The Glen'.'

Oh, where was that?

'At 'The Glen'; there's a garage there now. Mi daughter started work there when she wer sixteen and she still works fer the brewery now and she's over fifty. Ther was a fellow called Jimmy Law who had a farm at Stacksteads. It wer either 'Honeyhall' farm er 'Mitchell Nook' farm. He used to cart coal on his horse and cart down to Baxters Brewery at Waterfoot and Farholme Cotton Mill at that time.'

So he kept them going?

Yes. He wer carting coal all day to them two places.'

I suppose with all the pits round there'd be a lot of coalmen in Bacup. Can you remember the names of any?

'Oh yes, plenty. Hughie Waite; Bert Greenhalgh; Nuttalls; one chap called Atkinson up Weir Terrace; Sammy Falls; Co-op etc. Ther wer 'Hilltop Colliery' at Sharneyford. Rossendale Valley wer 'wick' wi pits and coalmen.'

Things have changed a lot now. People have gone on gas and electric and the young people wouldn't go in the pits today would they?

'You could go down Newchurch Road nearly every day and see women and children picking cinders out of the ashes at Plantation Mill. Some of them used to go all round the factories picking cinders.'

Tell me about this brewery at 'The Glen'; was it because of the water do you think?

'Well I've never tasted a better pint. Now what that wer because of – a don't know. Thi closed that brewery down though – I can't remember when.'

Well perhaps it had something to do with the water like the Whiskey Distillers in Scotland who use certain water.

'After 'Baxters' it wer 'Beverleys' and now it's 'Wilsons'. Our Rita worked there from being sixteen and now she's 52. She's worked there all her life.'

It amazes me what you can find in the Rossendale Valley.

'She could have been made redundant when they did away with that brewery at Waterfoot but she didn't; she kept travelling to Manchester every day; I think she's in the office at Halifax now. She learned to drive to go to work.'

So was your last job at the pit?

'Yes, 1968 at Easter I finished.'

And haven't you had your Diamond Wedding this year?

'No that's next year.'

Well I hope everyone remembers you. I'll have a word with Annie now. I'll come back to you after if you want to say anything else George.

ANNIE ORMEROD

'We'll have been married sixty year next year!'

Now Annie, where were you born and bred?

'Down Luke Street at Stacksteads, and I went to St. Joseph's School and I was in the Children of Mary when they used to carry the statue round the Church. Mi father paid 2/6d a week fer me to learn to weave at Atherton Holme. It's a slipper works now. Well when I got two looms when I'd been there twelve months, I got 10/- and I got 1d in the 1/- fer spending money off mi dad. Then I came up to Beech Mill after and we used to walk it from Stacksteads – me and

Annie Ormerod's store of memories encompasses sixty years of married life.

Mary Holt. We started work at 6 o'clock and we walked all the way from Stacksteads to Beech Mill and worked from 6am to 5.30pm and Saturday mornings – all fer 10/- a week!'

Yes, all for 10/-! Well, how did you come to meet George?

'I'll tell you how we met. There's a paper shop in Union Street, where the old Co-op is; near the Waterloo. The girls used to walk one way round the street and the boys walked the other way. They called it the 'Rabbit Run.'

I've heard of the 'Chicken Run' as well.

'Well we called it th' Rabbit Run. Anyway, ther wer him, and Arthur Kirby and Herbert Gerrard. They wer all stood together with Tommy Sellars. Ther wer me and Bessie Bellam – a friend; and these lads called of us. Anyway, they took us to the Empire and we went in the 'Monkey Rack'; 2d – and if a spotlight shone on you, you got 5/-! Anyway George asked me if I'd keep going and I wer courting wi him five years. Then wi got married and wi went living on Greenend Row belonging the Fibre Works; 2/6d a week rent; and then I'd been married ten years when our Colin wer born and I never had no more after that.'

You were saying about sheep's head broth?

'We used to get a sheep's head on the market at Saturday night fer 6d. Then we'd get a 'wrap-up' at Melia's fer a 1/- and then we'd go home and make a pan of broth.'

What was a wrap-up?

'A rabbit; 1lb carrots; 5lb potatoes; 1lb onions and a cabbage and you could go to the Maypole next to it and buy this pat o' butter er tub o' butter. Maypole was wer Home

Stores is now.'

So you didn't go out to work after you had Colin?

'Oh yes. There wer a woman up 'Plantation Back'; she wer a war widow; they called her 'Irish Pat'. She wer Lizzie Bullock on' she never had any children. She lost her husband in the first world war so she used to look after kiddies. I'd take Colin down at 6 o'clock of a morning when I worked at Paris Mill and she'd look after him. But if it were raining she'd keep him overnight. They always called her 'Nanny Bullock' and she was really good to the kids. You'd go in at dinnertime and you'd see all the little chairs round the table; you know sitting-up chairs. She loved all children. She was a nice woman. She only used to take about 2/6d a week off you. She was really good.'

How do you think Bacup's changed over the years?

'It's changed quite a lot, and for the worse I think. The shops aren't the same; there isn't the same variety now. Here where I live, they are good neighbours and the lady next door is 92 and she does all her own work; cooks all her meals and everything. She wer with me when I had Colin. She was born in that house; Mrs Ada Bolton she's called and she's still there 92 years later! She's marvellous!'

I was saying that a lot of people have never been down into Accrington.

'I had an auntie in Higher Antley Street so I used to go to Accrington – but not much.'

Buses go right there now, which I don't suppose they did then?

'They used to go to the Sacred Heart Church in Accrington. Aunt Biddie and mi Uncle Tommy worked at Howard and Bulloughs.

She was mi mother's sister. But you see when we were little mi mother left us and there were three of us. Mi dad had his leg took off in Ratcliffe's Quarry at Lee Mill and there wer no compensation then. I used to do the shopping fer an old lady at th' bottom called Molly Handley. She used to mek tea in a pan on the fire and she used to boil her tea. Johnny Woodruff came up one day and said to me: 'Molly wants you Annie.'

So I went down and there's this woman there with a long black skirt on and a black shawl. I said: 'What do you want Molly?'

She said: 'There's a lady here, don't you know her?' and I said: 'No I don'.'

She said: 'It's yer mother,' and I said: 'No it isn't.'

Were you the eldest Annie?

'Well, yes and I'd had everything to do when I come home from work; wash and bake and God knows what! And we had coal fires then wi th' oven and boilers.'

What about this woman that used to brew her tea on the fire?

'That was the old-fashioned way of brewing tea; to boil it in a pan on the fire. We had a pan with two handles on it and we'd boil our white clothes in it on the fire, on a kind of bracket that swung over the fire. On Friday we used to take the brass fire-irons and clean them and put them away till Sunday. We used to make peg rugs out of old jackets and coats. We used to get them off a woman called: 'Salt Emma'. She had a donkey in her house. She was a rag-woman and her real name was Emma Marsden.'

Were there a lot of rag and bone men round here?

'Oh yes; everyday! They'd come down th' street and you'd get a cob of salt er donkey stones; yellow stones etc.'

Do you remember any names? They used to collect jam jars as well didn't they?

'Oh yes, they'd collect jars. We got 1d for them at shops. Ther used to be some come from Burnley and Rawtenstall to do what we call 'Rag Tatting' round here. Mi father used to make us scrub the cellar steps; then we lived on a landing, and we'd all them steps to scrub besides.'

Well at least those things have changed for the better. You've a nice house – nice and comfortable aren't you?

'Yes. I wouldn't move. Our Colin's always saying: 'Why don't you get a bungalow?' But I wouldn't go. I'm here fer life.'

Well they've made the street look nice for you.

'Well that's Mrs Talukdar [a local councillor] – she's an angel! I met her one day over there and ther wer her and David Trippier; John Holt and Smith. And she says: 'Hello Annie, how are you going on?' – she always put her arm round me and asked me that. She was a lovely little person. Her husband's a doctor. I said: 'I'm fine – how are you?' She got the roads down for us, she deserves a gold medal.'

George: 'They talk about things changing for the better don't they? Well, from th' bottom of Todmorden Road to the Sharneyford boundary I could count 26 shops; there isn't one today!'

Were they pulled-down?

'Some have been pulled down but the others just closed. There used to be a pub down there and a ragchap called: Billy Gregson; he

wer a rag tatter!'

I suppose you've to go to the centre now?

'Yes we have. The pub was called: 'Green End Tavern' and ther wer an old fellow across the road used to fly pigeons. He used to train 'em fer pigeon flyers and they'd have dog trials at Sunday morning and greyhounds at the pub. It's a shop now!
Yes, they'd have a trail hunt the following Saturday with greyhounds. They'd have somebody with a rope and a rag and they'd douse this rag with aniseed and they'd go across the fields and when they went over a wall they'd bounce the rag on the wall. They went right round the moors and the dogs would follow the scent of the aniseed.
They were happy days up here then, but since all that went it's not been the same. It's very quiet up here. You could be dead and buried up here and nobody would know. And we don't 'neighbour' in and out your house. There's none of that. But if you're ill they're marvellous. They're really good neighbours fer that.'

Is there anything else you want to tell me. It's been very interesting listening to you.

'I'd rather listen to a record than watch television. We get that much rubbish. We used to have a radiogram but we gave it away at finish – I like Coronation Street and darts and snooker though.'

George: 'I used to have a gramophone with barrel records. You had to push it on a kind of sleeve.'

Have you still got it?

'No I haven't. I did know a couple who had one a few years ago; but whether they still have it, I don't know. It would be worth something

today.'

I can remember 'His Masters Voice'.

Annie: 'Oh yes with the big horn!'

George: 'Yes, we've had one of them before the radiogram. First wireless we had at 1/- a week wer shaped like a cone, and you hung it on the wall. We were the first up here to have one. It was the Relay fer 1/- a week!'

Is the Co-op still here in Bacup?

Annie: 'Well they've had a new one built; it's down Irwell Street now.'

George: 'We used to have one at the bottom of here; one at Britannia; one at Weir Terrace; one at Lee Mill; one at Stacksteads etc. And where you go up them steps there used to be a grocer's shop at the bottom, besides the Co-op. There's one chap at Stacksteads and he's still going yet and he's been going fifty-odd years up by the Hare and Hounds Garage!'

George and Annie are very content and live very comfortably in the little house they've had for fifty years. I hope they enjoy their diamond wedding next year.

Maggie Edwards
of Bacup

'I was born in Shepherd Street, Bacup. I went to Bank School as a young child then to Mount School up Lanehead Lane. I went half time at twelve years old learning to weave at Elm Brothers Mill. Mi mother finished at Christmas to have another baby which was born in January and I left the mill as well as I was getting no pay as a learner! I then went to J. Hoyle's India Mills for a time. In 1914 the man I was 'tenting' for on six looms was called up in the army so I-got two looms on mi own and I was now earning a wage. The man I had been working with used to give me a threepenny bit every week. I always put it in mi clog and one day it stuck to mi stocking and I lost it. However, mi mother found it and I got thumped fer not telling her I had it. We started work at 5.30am with no lights in the street. We used to meet the lamplighter in the Bacup streets with his long pole which he used to pull the gas tap on. I was often frightened going out in the dark but sometimes a neighbour waited for mi and I went down with him. This lad was eighteen when he was called up; he was sent to Mesopotamia and he never came back. Later I got four looms at Meadows Mill where I stayed fer a few years. We had to move from one mill to another then, when work was scarce. Sometimes we had a long way to walk so we went on the tram (steam tram) when we could. If we went to Burnley we had to walk; the trams only ran as far as Rawtenstall.'

Can you tell me what Bacup was like then, when you were young?

'Oh, there was a smashing market then! There was a market hall at the top of the hill and open-air stalls on the roadside past St. Mary's. The stalls had meat; fruit; fish; tripe; everything you could think of or need. When the 'divi' from the Co-op was due, the people went to the market and they had a 'real good do.' The women bought curtain material; they were very clean about themselves and their homes, oh yes – very particular they were. Let me tell you; you would *never* see a line of washing out on a Sunday! The steps were always scrubbed as well.'

What did you do for entertainment in Bacup when you were in your teens?

'Well I was a Sunday School scholar and I liked that. At 'Ebenezer' we had a good choir too. Most of the chapels are closed now though, isn't that awful?'

Where did you go for a holiday?

'I never had one. I was seventeen before I even saw the sea! I went fer five days and I had thirty shillings which had to pay fer a bed (two shillings a night); tenpence if two of us slept together – so I only had to pay a shilling. This holiday was what you called 'apartments'. You provided the food and the landlady cooked what you wanted and you slept there. I took three eggs; some butter; a tin of salmon; two tins of fruit and some cheese with mi. I also had to pay fer vegetables and the cruet. I was with a man and wife and their daughter who was mi friend, so I had to pay mi share fer meat er fish or whatever we had. The train fare was half a crown [12½p]. I kept a shilling to pay to go into the tower. There wer no money fer ice-cream; even had there been any. It was 1917 and there wasn't enough food let alone ice-cream!'

How many had you in the family?

'There wer six children and mi mother owned the house across the street which she bought fer £100. When it wer pulled down she got £7,000! Mi father worked hard fer his children. He was a quiet man; but mi mother was bad to live with. It's not surprising though is it – going out to work and having six children. She wer allus tired out. I wanted to sit fer a scholarship but mother said that I couldn't go to the Grammar School even if I passed; she wanted mi wage. We looked after her as well as we could when she was older but she led us a dog's life fer years!'

Did you go to Accrington at all?

'Very seldom. I worked on a greengrocer's stall every Saturday, so never got out a lot.'

You go to the Trinity Methodist Chapel now, don't you?

'Yes, it cost about £13,000 to convert from a Sunday School and it's very good.'

Are you a member of any pensioners' groups in Bacup?

'Oh yes I joined one once. I used to make jam and cakes to sell and help with raffles to raise funds.'

What did you do in the second world war?

Maggie Edwards has spent almost all of her 93 years in Bacup.

from other windows I saw when I was out. Mi fathers' parents lived until their late Eighties. Their doctor said he couldn't understand this because they ate all the wrong kinds of food, but I said they had to eat what they could get! Mi mother used to make broth with a sheep's head, we also had cowheel and trotters – all good warming food; fresh not frozen! I lived in Manchester fer about four years and I got along with the people very well but I preferred Bacup.

I met a lady who came from a family who sold material on the market in Manchester. Twice in the year they took so much money they didn't know what to do with it! (This was from another stall they had on Bacup market!!)'

Maggie still lives in Bacup and is obviously very fond of it. She is a marvellous old lady with a still lively mind and was very good to talk to.

'Well, when we got this house we had nothing. We couldn't buy lino er carpet and black-out was the only kind of curtaining; so I crotcheted lace curtains fer five windows. I used to copy a pattern

Bill Mellor
Clog Maker

Clog making is a dying art. There are very few cloggers left today in any Lancashire town. At one time though, even places like Bacup and Oswaldtwistle had several cloggers and shoe repairers. Is it because our shoes are made of plastic or synthetic substances now that we don't need these talented men any more? Or is it that people just don't take as much care in their choice of shoes and looking after their feet? I only know that there are only one or two clog makers left, and I was lucky enough to trace and be able to speak to a few of them, including Bill Mellor:

'I was born in Waterfoot and I went to Whitewell Bottom council school. When I left school I worked in a slipper factory before joining the army. After the war I started my own business as a clogger in Bacup, Lancashire.'

How did you learn the trade?

'Well I trained with the bloke I met in the army and he showed me what to do. He was from Northampton. Then I trained with an old clogger I met up here in Bacup. He was over seventy years old; Harry Pilling was his name. I started up in 1950.'

Were you actually making clogs or just repairing them?

'Yes, I made clogs; at least I made the uppers that is. We bought the wooden soles ready-made from a factory. Very few cloggers made the soles as they took a long time to make and we could buy machine made ones reasonable like. You could alter them a size or so though, one way or the other. In time we had to buy leather in bulk so it was cheaper to buy the uppers then.

I used to make clogs for St. Mary's Clog Dancers of Oswaldtwistle. Mrs Hindle was the leader and they always came to me. I could supply them with clogs of all kinds. I'm retiring when this property is demolished; it's condemned. [This is his shop in Yorkshire Street, Bacup.] There are others who say they can take over but I don't know. Trade is going down; people don't have shoes repaired now as they used to. They buy cheap shoes and throw them away when they are worn. A new pair of clogs costs about £36.50 now, which people won't pay. Once upon a time I used to buy a lot of clogs made-up. I sold them at 14/11 [75p]. I bought these ready-made clogs from a place in Yorkshire. I put a pair in the shop window to show. Lorry drivers used to come this way from Yorkshire and they bought clogs from me, saying they couldn't get them in Yorkshire! I took this shop over from Horace Bradshaw, who has since died.'

St. James's Square, Bacup, in the 1950s.

Do you think clogs are better for the feet?

'Oh yes. There are doctors who send children fer clogs when they have foot problems. Clogs are more firm, so the foot is better supported. People come here from Rochdale, Halifax, all over the place and I have a pair here for the Isle of Man. When I retire people will have to go to Rawtenstall fer shoe repairs then.'

Indeed, Bill has retired since I spoke to him, which leaves Bacup without a clogger. He has been sorely missed for his skills and knowledge of the clog trade.

Three Lancashire Tales

A True Tale about an 'Eggcup'

A Rossendale woman was born into a very poor family on a farm above the Bacup Moors some seventy years ago. The mother left her and her two brothers of four and five, when she was three months old. Grandma was brought in to look after the family. They were so poor they only had two eggcups which were always given to the boys. The little girl used to cry about this, but to no avail.

One day, when she was four, they were having eggs for tea and she cried as usual because she'd no eggcup. Her father, a collier, came through the door and asked: 'What's thee shriekin about again?' 'I've no eggcup,' the child sobbed. 'We'll sort that out then – I'm sick of 'earin thi shriekin.'

Her father went to the fireplace, took the poker, pushed it into the fire, and left it to get as hot as it could. Then he took the red hot poker back to the wooden table and burnt a hole right through it, thrusting the poker into the wood. He stood back, looked at the hole, and said, 'There's thi bloody eggcup; nah stop shriekin wilta?'

Another Lancashire Tale

A lady I spoke to was the eldest of fourteen children. Her mother was *very* harassed, and by the time baby number eleven came along she used to tell her eldest daughter to keep the younger ones out of her way. 'She didn't mind what I did, as long as the kids wer out from under her feet,' said Rose. 'So I had to think of something good when ther wer seven or eight kids muckin' about. First I put two er three in the dolly tub, then if thi wer small enough, I tied a few on't rack and pulled id up good. Them as wer left, I get ther shirt laps er pinnies and caught 'em int'mangle rollers then thi couldn't move so far then.'

It would appear that the old saying 'Necessity is the mother of invention' certainly applied here.

Another use for the Dolly Tub

A women aged 86 from up the valley told me, 'When't war were on a wer freet'nd to deeath. A used to run in't pantry, put mi head in't dolly tub an wait theear till thid finished droppin' them theer INDECENT bombs.'

Doing the washing and minding the baby in Back Ashmount, Cloughfold in 1959.

The Britannia Coconut Dancers

No book or anthology on Rossendale would be complete without a mention of the famous Coconutters of Bacup. For many years these black-faced men have delighted Valley residents and visitors alike with their unusual and exotic appearance in their performance of the unique coconut dance. They have traditionally performed in Bacup on Easter Saturday every year, and are also popular participants in local carnivals and charity events.

Much has been said and written about the Coconutters, but I was privileged to interview a member who has been associated with them for almost thirty years and, indeed is still dancing with them. Mr. Brian Daley told me of his experiences with these fine dancers, and also quite a bit about his life in Bacup itself.

Brian was born in Bacup in 1930, and went to St. Mary's R.C. school; then at fourteen he went as an apprentice sheet metal worker at Lea Mill in Bacup. I asked him how he came to get involved with the Coconut Dancers, and this is what he said:

'Well, I'd always been interested and followed the group, but they disbanded during the war. They started up again in 1947. I was seventeen then and still used to watch them on Easter Saturday, as my eldest brother was a member. Four of them came up to dance for mi mother, because she couldn't go to see them. The band played outside and the dancers came into the house to dance. We had no carpets then, just a lino floorcovering. Anyhow, I got married in 1951 and went living up Britannia. I'd never had any thoughts about joining the dancers, but I saw an advert in the *Bacup Times* saying that they wanted a learner. They used to practise in the Britannia Working Men's Club a few nights each week, or so.'

Why were they called Coconut Dancers?

'Nobody really knows. Historians claim that the dance and the dress had its origins in the Moorish pirates who brought the dance into Cornwall sometime during the seventeenth century. The tin miners came to work in the quarries which stretched the full length of the Rossendale Valley and they brought the dance with them. The dance has never been done outside the Rossendale Valley.'

How long have you been a member?

'Twenty-nine years. We do a lot for charity and are always being asked to dance at carnivals and fairs.'

Tell me about the dress. It's very unusual, isn't it?

'Well, we wear a black polo-neck sweater, a white kilt with three red bands on, and the bottom of the kilt is just above the knee. Black velvet knee breeches, white stockings and Lancashire clogs. The hat is made of white linen, with ribbons and pom-poms, rosettes and a feather at the front. A zig-zag ribbon runs around the edge of the hat – red ribbon for a gent and blue for a lady. The kilt has a strap worn over the left shoulder for a lady and the right shoulder for a gent. At one time only men were folk and morris dancers, but now there are women's teams starting up. We have no ladies in the Coconutters as yet. We have twelve members at present, but only eight dance at one time.'

You blacken your face, too, I believe?

'Yes, we blacken our faces, and the reason for this is that the dance goes back to pagan times and a black face is a disguise so that the spirits don't know the dancer. Even today the natives in the Brazilian jungle disguise the face when doing a ritual dance. They paint their faces white.'

What do you use to blacken your face?

Not long before I joined they were still using soot and lard. Some preferred burnt cork, but now we use theatrical make-up. Some people say the earlier troupes used lamp-black for years. Easter Saturday has been the traditional day for the dance as long as anyone can remember. We used to dance on Good Friday, but only in Ramsbottom. This was discontinued because if it rained on Good Friday the garlands got wet and we didn't look at our best on Easter Saturday.'

Have the Coconutters appeared on television?

Yes, over twenty-odd times, dancing with the team. We dance at Whitworth rush-bearing ceremony every year on the first Friday in September as well. Saddleworth also has a rush-bearing ceremony at which we dance. When the rush is paraded through the village, there will be twenty different teams of folk dancers. The rush is about forty feet high and a man sits on the top. People are often puzzled as to why a dance like ours has survived all these years in a small industrial town like Bacup, with a population around sixteen thousand. It's one of the oldest, if not the oldest, dance in the British Isles.'

Why do you think it has survived then?

'Well, it seems to be handed down from father to son and also there has been no outside influence. The members have always been dancers – we've never had a non-dancing manager. All decisions are taken by vote. I remember four brothers who were all members, I had a brother and two brothers-in-law who were all in, and I think that's what keeps it going. There are no written instructions about the dance – members have to learn the steps and remember them. Every movement and step in the dance has a name – e.g. when the dance starts off, there's the gallop round, then there's advance and dummy jumping up, jumping down, under th'head etc. Every movement takes one bar of music. When you're learning, you know the steps and have to learn the name of the movement to follow the progress of the dance.'

Has Bacup changed over the years?

'Yes, it has changed, it's changed a lot. I think one thing to cause this was the moving of the market down into the town centre. During and after the war there was an indoor market which was a very good one, and a big one. The character of the town seemed to change after the move. We don't see the same individual characters either, that I remember as a teenager. There was one they called 'Robert the Devil'. He was a market labourer. He used to clean up around the stalls and work as a general dogsbody. A woman once asked him if he'd take a sewing machine from Bacup up to Britannia. It was one of the old types of treadle machines on wheels, and he shoved it all the way up there. He got to Britannia and the woman gave him sixpence. He says: 'If that's all th' t'goina gimme, I'll tek id back,' and he wheeled it all the way back down again!'

How many cloggers are left in Bacup?

None now, I think. When my clogs need repairing I've to go to

Todmorden because my dancing clogs have very pointed toes. Dandy clogs or Sunday clogs, they are called. I got a pair in 1958 and they're still like new. I have another pair that I bought from a retiring manager. He'd had them twenty-odd years and they were secondhand when he got them from an uncle who'd also got them secondhand. I've had them since 1960 so they must be seventy years old and they're still in regular use.

I've danced at the Albert Hall five times and we've also been to the international Eisteddfod at Llangollen. The Coconut dance is a definite folk dance which means that the dance originated in your own region. We don't do anybody else's dances. Morris dancers do dances from other regions, but not folk dancers like us.'

It made fascinating listening to hear Brian's enthusiasm and affection for the Britannia Coconutters. They work so hard and are so dedicated to their cause that they deserve all the support t they can get. Many in Rossendale would be dismayed if this tradition were not carried on and I hope they'll have many more successful years.

Sadly, Brian has died since this interview; a great loss to the dancers.

Elizabeth Chattwood
of Edenfield

I have come to speak to Elizabeth Chattwood who has lived in Edenfield for 83 years. And have you always lived in the same house?

'No, I lived at the Guide Post. I was born in a house up East Street opposite the church, but we lived at the Guide Post for 22 years. I have lived here in Market Street since 1937/8.'

So where were you actually born?

'I was born in East Street.'

And what about schooling?

'I went to the little school there – Edenfield School – it was a very good school, as it is to this day.'

Can you remember any of the teachers?

'Yes, Miss Haworth and Miss Hilary. Mr. Greenwood was the headmaster and there was also Mr. Parkin; I liked Mr. Parkin. I went to school when I was three. I had

six brothers all older than me and they all went there too.'

Were you the only girl then?

'No, my sister was the eldest, then my six brothers and then me, and a very happy family we were too.'

Are any of your brothers or sister still living?

'No, I'm the only one left. I'm the youngest and the only one living.'

How old were you when you left the Edenfield School?

'I was fourteen and went to the same school until I left.'

And what was your first job on leaving school?

'I went as a nursemaid to some people in Ramsbottom. After that I went learning to weave – which I didn't like. My mother didn't want me to go weaving but in those days there was nothing else. I went to Alty's at the bottom of Bury Road; not a big place but a very happy

place. I stayed there until they closed down 23 years ago.'

Can you tell me a bit about the village of Edenfield?

'Well, there were characters who came through, but there's none left today; in fact I don't know everybody across the way. At one time we knew everybody in the village and all the shops as well. In fact, from the Guide Post (this being by the church where the road divides); I used to live in the first house at Blackburn Road; and there were only three houses altogether and from the Guide Post to the Market Place there were 28 shops.'

Were some of them house shops – you know, in their front rooms?

'No, they were proper shops. There was a confectioner's lower down from here, and we had four cobblers who made clogs.'

Can you remember any of their names?

'Well, one was Bob Shore's, where the library was at one time, they made shoes and sold shoes. Then there was the Co-op, the first shop in the block there; they sold shoes and made clogs, and then there was one at the Market Place where Pat has her hairdressing now. He was a deaf and dumb man; a very nice man and he just repaired shoes; he

Looking towards Rochdale down St. James's Street, Bacup in 1900.

was called Lord.'

Funnily enough there was a man in Accrington who was deaf and dumb and he was a shoemaker and clog-maker, but he was called Walmsley.

'This man only repaired shoes, he didn't make clogs, but he was a very pleasant man. All those small shops made a living but of course there were no supermarkets then like there are today. I prefer the little shops myself, today there is no atmosphere and you don't get the same service!'

What other kind of shops were there?

'There was one across from the church which was a sweet shop and general store and years later part of it was made into a chip shop. There was one next to the Conservative Club where I think they made chips at one time; then there was the first shoe shop and then, higher up near the Co-op where those new houses have been built, across from the doctor's surgery, in that row there was a painter's and decorator's, and everyone went there for their wallpaper.'

Did it become Taylor's later?

'Yes it did. Didn't they move to St. Annes?'

Yes, in fact I went to see Minnie Taylor a short while ago; she is in a nursing home at Blackpool. Her husband died. They had a son called Peter who lives in Bury.

'If you ever go to see her again remember me to her, she knows me well enough.

Now as I was saying, there was the painter's and decorator's and next to that was a barber's shop, one next to that had two windows and that's now the doctor's surgery. It was a milliner's at one time and they made hats. The lady who made them was called Eliza Wolstenholme, she was always very busy at Whitsuntide making hats for walking day. Later on at the end of that row was a ladies' dress shop. Then across the road was the Co-op, the building is still there. Then there was the shoe shop; the one with the two windows was a big grocer's shop and next door was a draper's shop. Lower down on the same side there was another ladies' outfitters; Mrs. Elton's. Across the road, just past the Bank was Chattwood's drapers (same name as me), that's now an antique shop!'

Were they any relation?

'Very distant, if any, I don't know what it was.

Then there was the paper shop which is still there but has been extended. We didn't have a chemist in those days. Then there was a little confectioner's lower down and at the top of Park Road there was a little shop that Jim Haworth had; nobody could carve boiled ham like Jim Haworth, he was an artist at it.'

Did he cure his own?

'I think he must have done. He was a great big fellow and always had a nice smock on and a white apron and he always had a cap on too. He had some rooms down Park Road and he let the lads of the village go in to play dominoes; I don't think they had darts in those days. I don't think there was anywhere else for them to go.

Then there was a butcher's shop there, but the only one I can remember having it was a chap called Elton, and I was grown up then. Then the sweet shop was owned by somebody called Elsby. Across the road where Dorothy Kershaw's shop was – I was very sad when that closed – that was Chattwood's grocer's shop; the same people who had the draper's shop. The mother and one daughter were in the grocer's shop and another daughter was in the draper's. Next door to there, which

is now a little office of some kind, that used to be a grocer's shop; you know, who used to be Heys in Rawtenstall, Bank Street; a high class grocer's – well, they used to have that shop there. Then the confectioner's, Sixsmith's, is still there. A Mrs. Gee had it at one time years and years ago, and of course Fishers had it for a long time. Next door to there, was a little shop (I think two sisters lived there) and they always called it 'Annie-Libby's'; I think one of them taught young women to embroider and things like that. Next door was the shoe shop, Lord's.'

So it was a good community, you wouldn't need to go out of the village for anything, would you?

'No, as I said, there were 28 shops.'

Yes, it is important that we should get it down because people soon forget. You were saying that you had a lot of characters in the village – can you remember any of those?

'I remember one man who came, they called him 'Salt Sammy', he frightened me to death – he used to carry a sack on his back and when they said, 'Salt Sammy's coming,' we used to fly; I suppose he was alright really!'

Did he get that name because he sold salt?

'No, he was a rag gatherer. I can't remember any more; my friend should be here from across the road, we were brought up together since we wer three.'

And what is she called?

'Ellen Haworth, she has a better memory than me, she remembers many things that I can't.'

Was there anyone who came round selling things like lamp-oil etc.?

'There was a man used to come round; I think he came from Manchester, he was a Jew and I think he used to sell ladies' clothing and things, and he came for quite a number of years.

I always remember the haymakers. There was a man who came year after year, a decent man, he was called Mark Common and he used to haymake for Whittakers over at Crowwood's.

I remember the gipsies who used to come, we never got to know the gipsies personally but we got to know them by sight. Some of them were quite decent people. I remember there was once a gipsy baby christened at the church, and they called her Phoebe James, I suppose James was her surname.'

Did they come in caravans, and where did they put them?

'Going down by the bridge where the tip was, they would put them on there. Sometimes they stayed for weeks on end but they were decent people and never caused any trouble.'

There wouldn't be any main lights up here when you were young, would there?

'I can't remember that, I'm afraid. I can remember the Market Place – it used to be called the 'Big Lamp'. You know where the junction is between Rochdale Road and Bury Road, and in the middle of the road was a big lamp and it used to be a meeting place for some of the lads at night.'

Has there ever been a market in Edenfield?

'Well, I've never known it, though they've always called it the Market Place.'

There's two or three pubs here, aren't there?

'Yes, there's the Pack Horse – at least, it was the Pack Horse, but they've changed the name and I can't remember what it's called but it's across from the Coach and Horses. Then there's the Horse and Jockey and the Rostron's Arms, and there used to be one called the Volunteer but I don't remember it. Then there was the Bird in Hand up the street up Gin Croft Lane. There used to be one down Blackburn Road called the Horseshoe.'

There wouldn't be a lot of entertainment in Edenfield so I suppose people went to the pubs to socialise.

'Well, we went to the Sunday Schools, you know. I went to the Methodists near the Market Place which was pulled down; there's a bungalow there now. I go to the Methodists on Rochdale Road now.'

And of course, there's the Parish Church.

'Oh yes, we always supported the Parish Church as well as our own.'

They'll have their walking days, I suppose, even yet.

'Yes, they still have their walking days but we don't now at the Methodists. They have some very good workers at the church. It's a lovely little church, have you been in it? Incidentally, we were all christened there, so I believe.'

Did you ever go on Sunday School trips?

No, I'm afraid I didn't join in a lot of things when I was young, but I've made up for it lately.'

Did you go to Ramsbottom to do your shopping?

'Rawtenstall. My mother used to go to the market there and she had to walk to Ewood Bridge to get the train with these women on Thursday nights which were market nights and then they would have to walk back again with what they had bought.'

What about the winters up here? I bet you've had some bad ones.

'Rather, I will show you some photographs.'

(Miss Chattwood is showing me some photos of New Hall.) Where would this be?

'Well, you go up Gin Croft and there's the water works up there, and now there's a bungalow where this New Hall was. At one time I think there was someone called Rostron lived there.'

Well looking at it, I am sure somebody rich lived there.

'I also have a photo of the Conservative Club when it was opened in 1905, there they are with their tall hats on.'

t's nice to have these things to remember days gone by. (She is now showing me pictures of the snow in the winters of 1947/48. It is piled up against the telegraph poles.) I remember the winter of '47 but I believe 1940 was an even worse winter. I can remember some people who have grown up in the village. Do you remember a Mr. Hanna?**

'Yes, though I didn't know him personally. I know Isabel his daughter, though.'

A Mr. Barker? He used to grow nice flowers.

'No I didn't know him, but I have heard of him. He had a lovely garden.'

Can you tell me about the Community Centre. Now it's used for all kind of activities isn't it?

'Oh, yes though I can't tell you much about it because I'm not connected with it. I haven't joined because I'm against it or anything, but I'm President of the Women Conservatives; I've been going to the Conservative Club since I was sixteen. I used to be secretary to what they used to call the 'Imps' in those days; the young Conservatives. They called them the Junior Imperial League in those days. Yes, I have a lot of memories, on the political side. And I'm a member of the W.I. in Turn. I like the W.I. but I've missed a lot this last year due to ill-health.'

You are managing to keep warm are you? These are good stone-built houses aren't they, and you have a lovely view at the back?

'Yes I have, and though I like travelling I have no desire to live anywhere else, I love Edenfield!'

Do you ever go to Ramsbottom or Rawtenstall much these days?

'No, it's very rare I go to Ramsbottom but I go to Rawtenstall to Kwiksave and I come straight back. I go to Bury market sometimes, it's a good market but the bus fares are pretty stiff, even though we get half fare it costs us a pound to go. But it is a good market, especially the fruit section!'

Mrs. Fisher has been up here a long time. (Jenny Fisher on Market Street.)

'I think she was born here, I can remember her when she was a little girl.'

There used to be a Mrs. French

'Yes, she lived across the road. Her house and the one next door were pulled down and that new one was built. She died four years ago, there aren't many of the original 'Edenfieldites' left now.'

There was Amos Taylor, who's still here isn't he?

'He was brought up at Irwell Vale.'

What about Elsie Whittaker, I believe she's a right 'Edenfieldite'.

'I know Elsie, but she wasn't born here. She came here when she was very young, though.'

She's alright is Elsie, a very good worker for the church!

What a pleasure it was to speak to this charming old lady who has done so much for the community over the years in the village of Edenfield.

Maggie Shore of Ramsbottom

Maggie Shore outside her shop at 1, Carr Street, Ramsbottom in about 1929.

'I was born across the way in Spring Street, where I lived until I was nine. We then went to Oswaldtwistle for two years, because my father got work there. We then came back to Ramsbottom and I've lived here ever since. I went to St. Joseph's school as a child as I was a Catholic and my parents insisted I went to a Catholic school even though there was a school at the bottom of the street'.

Why was that?

'Because it was a Protestant school and there was much bigotry in those days between different religions'.

Did you wear clogs for school?

'Of co'oarse I did, and I went through all the classes wearin 'em. I enjoyed mi school days, so I went until I wer fourteen. I left school then and went as an apprentice milliner. I worked two years fer nothing just to serve an apprenticeship then I started on the 'handsome' wage of four shillings [20p] per week. I did all mi own hats so I saved money that way. I later started mi own business in a shop at the Market Place at Ramsbottom. Everybody knew me as 'Maggie' then.
Millinery was a good business in the summer, but in the winter there was nothing doing. Mi mother couldn't afford to keep me, so I had to leave, and I started working in the drapery trade. I was there four years, and I then decided to work for miself, so I took mi own shop, in Bridge Street. Later I moved to a shop where the Doctor's Clinic is. I sold all sorts there; from a Beechams Pill to a pair of silk stockings. Mi daughter Margaret was five when we went in there. I served in the Co-op grocer's during the First World War as well.'

What entertainment was there in Ramsbottom when you were young?

'Well we played hide-and-seek; skipping rope; bat and ball etc. There's none of that now. When we got two picture places in Ramsbottom we thought we were everybody, and now we've nothing. I never went out with a boy until I was eighteen because I wasn't allowed to (mi mother wouldn't let mi). If he wasn't a Catholic that didn't suit either. My husband wasn't a Catholic but he 'turned' fer me. We had a very happy marriage, but he died when he was only sixty, so I've been a widow ever since. I'm still 'batting' yet though and I haven't a stiff joint in mi body.'

What do you attribute that to?

'I'm not sure but I don't 'drink'; I think I'll celebrate mi 91st birthday with a Guinness.'

Did you have your shop when you were married then Maggie?

'Yes, where the clinic is now. My shop was next to the library and I sold all sorts. I was open anytime in the morning until anytime at night. There were no fixed hours, and it wer seven days a week; you closed when thi last customer had gone! Sometimes customers knocked on the door at 10 p.m. if they wanted something and I allus served them.

I still belong to St. Joseph's church. I'm a devoted R.C., and will be until I die. We were skitted [scorned] and called all kinds of things because we were Roman 'Ca'a'thlics', but I loved mi church and I love it still. I haven't been well enough to go this last few months, but the ['Blessed Sacrament'] communion is brought to me every Sunday. I think that's wonderful, I really do!

I knew everybody in Ramsbottom; having a shop brings you in contact with lots of people. I sold everything; dolly blue fer washing; hair-nets; cough bottles and all kinds of drinks (non-alcoholic of course!). If I didn't

A recent view of Bolton Road, Ramsbottom, from the Market Place.

have in stock what a customer wanted I went to Manchester for it.

People 'call' the Jews but I always found them very honest. I paid cash to them and often made a hundred per cent profit on what I bought. (I can say that now because not many of my former customers are still alive.)'

How did you travel to Manchester?

'Well, my husband worked on the railway so I got concessionary travel then.'

Have you any family?

'Yes I have a daughter Margaret, in Ramsbottom; and three grandchildren. I often wish I'd had more children though, they're so lovely.'

Did you have any holidays?

'No, I never closed the shop, and anyway I had mi mother with mi till she was 84. I had mi shop nine years then, when I was forty I retired. I'd made enough then so I bought this house and settled down.'

Was there a market in Ramsbottom?

'Yes, every Saturday; it opened at 12 o'clock. Thi had a 'penny stall' and you could buy all sorts fer a penny then. For sixpence – oh, you could get God knows what, fer sixpence!'

How has Ramsbottom changed since you were a girl?

'Oh it's changed a great deal; sometimes I think for the better, sometimes I wish it hadn't changed at all. People were more honest than they are now. I hadn't a lot of 'tick' [credit] but I had some good honest customers. I used to take £5 or £10 when I went to Manchester and I could buy all sorts. When I started in business I had £100 which I spent on stock, and within twelve months I had it back, and a shop full of 'stuff' as well. The secret of business is to be able to talk to people and to know who you can trust. I go to the hostel on Bolton Road West on a Monday for lunch and tea.'

Did you have a fair come to Ramsbottom?

'Yes, we used to go on the swings and make ourselves sick. The fairground was down where the 'tram' shed is now. Trams used to go from Edenfield to Bury for sixpence [2½p]. Of course, thirty bob [shillings – £1.50p] a week was a good wage in those days.'

What about going for walks to Peel Tower and Holcombe?

'Oh, we hadn't to do that on Good Friday as Catholics. No, that was a sin; a mortal sin! I never liked crowds anyway; I liked to be where it was quiet.'

Did you have a 'walking day'?

'Oh yes, every Whit Saturday. The Protestants walked at Friday and the Catholics and New Jerusalem walked at Saturday.'

Did you go to dances?

'Oh, I danced till I wer' eighty. We had dances every week at St Joseph's and we also went to the Conservative Club to dances. I could have re-married twice since I was widowed, but I wasn't having three men chasing me on the 'Last Day'; not likely! I question some parts of my faith, but, I always say: 'I go to church to worship God, not the priests or the building.' Times have changed, I worked in the Co-op, at one time and we worked every day from 8 a.m. to 8 p.m., 9.30 p.m. on a Friday and 10.30 on a Saturday.'

Were there any cloggers in Ramsbottom?

'Oh yes, the Shaw family were clog makers. They had a cloggers' shop up Edenfield but I don't think there are any left now.'

Did you have coal fires then?

'Yes; when I think about chopping wood to get a fire going and all the coal dust and ashes, I couldn't do it

now! I'd much rather press a switch!

When you started courting and went out on a Friday night, that meant that you were going to get married. All in all, I think the old days were better, we weren't out late like they are to-day, aye – crumbs! We had to 'tip all our wages up' and get one penny fer every shilling to spend. We had to save up out of that when we were going to get married as well.'

You do have a T.V. for company though?

'Yes, but that's a time-waster, and that's where the young people get all their information from. It's wrong all the stuff that's on there! Some mothers don't care what their children do so long as they can do as they like. There's no discipline to-day, we daren't say 'boo to a goose' in my day.'

When I spoke to Maggie, quite some time ago now, she was still at her home in Stanley Street. Now, she isn't quite as well, so she's at Hollymount Hostel. Certainly she seems to have been quite a strong character, and lots of people I spoke to remembered her and her shop. I'm glad I was able to speak to her whilst she was still at home. 'Well done Maggie – 93 and not-out!'.

Jim Welding
1897–1990

Looking at Jim's forehead – he'd hardly a line there – I said he must have had a 'charmed' life. 'Not really – it's been a hard life,' he replied.

'I wer' born and bred at St. Helens and went to school there. I allus wanted to be an engineer though, but when I wer' sixteen and a half years old, First World War broke out, so I joined the Royal Engineers, but I didn't get sent abroad – I wer' too young. Anyway, we wer' sent to mek camps fer the troops, fer the recruits. I worked at Pilkington's Glass works half time when I wer' twelve, and they had the'r own schools, fire brigade, doctors etc. – they had everything that wer' needed. I also used to do running as well when I wer' young. I wer' in the Territorial Army when war wer' declared and they sent us to Barrow-in-Furness.

After the war, mi mother wer'

living at Summerseat and I still wanted engineering, so I worked on the railway then and lived with her. Trains wer' running then to Bacup and Accrington. I used to go to Manchester on Saturday night and sleep in the First Class carriages, then Sunday morning we wer' up at 6 a.m. laying tracks. Railway wer' important in them days. There wer' plenty of horses in Summerseat then – everything wer' brought by them. Summerseat wer' a lovely little place though, and when I wer' older, I went to the Conservative Club and ended up as chairman there. I wer' also on a lot of village committees and charities in the village etc. About this time I got married and went living back in St. Helens, and worked at Pilkington Brothers' Colliery, but in 1921 the pit strike started, so I came back to work at Ramsbottom. I wer' a steel erector in the army, so in 1921, the Ocean

Chemical Company wer' just being built here at Ramsbottom, and I got a job with Booth's contractors working on the distillation plant here down Nuttall Lane. Well, the engineer in charge of the works must have been watching me and just as I wer' finishing the steel erector's job, he asked me to work for him, putting up the chemical company. Money and everything wer' alright, but I wer' living in St. Helens and I'd to get from there to Ramsbottom every day. A friend who was an Insurance Agent offered to lend me his bike, and I'd to sign on the back of his photograph '1/- on account' – in case I had an accident. I still have that photograph yet!

Whilst in Summerseat I wer' chairman of the 'Victories' committee after the Second World War as well. I've a photo here of Nuttall Hall Farm just across the fields here. Anyway, to get back to 1921 – I used this bike fer about six months, and bikes were hard work then; they weren't like they are today. I set off at 5 o'clock each morning to cycle to Ramsbottom, and the offices wer' in this house here – my house I'm in now – it belonged to the Ocean Chemical Company. I started living here in 1952 when we closed down. It took me two hours to cycle here and I'd start work at 7.15 a.m. exactly!'

You must have been fit!

'I wer'! But then I found a house in Summersseat and I became manager of the Ocean Chemical Company from about 1948 until it closed in 1952. I only really retired at 83 though, because when the chemical works closed, I'd to look fer another job. Anyway, I knew a lot of people and got on at the local soap works in Kenyon Street, but it wasn't really what I wanted. Part of Ocean Chemicals wer' run as a bleaching works after 1952 and I ran that for a bit – about two years, but when that shut, that wer' when I went to the soap works. Then I

Grant's Arms, Ramsbottom.

went to Turnbull and Stockdale at Rosebank, Ramsbottom – Stubbins, actually, and I wer' there as Maintenance Engineer until 1980. I retired twice really – thi wanted me to stop at the works, but I wer' getting on and asked to retire, so thi bought me a clock. Anyway, I wer' only at home ten days and I wer' fed up, so I went back again fer a bit, and manager said, 'Well, when you do finish, you can't have another clock!'.

Ramsbottom wer' a grand little place though. We had *every* trade you could want – ther' wer' a mill across here near where I live – Nuttall Mill, started by the Grant brothers – and ther' wer' trains running all over t'place! I've always drunk spring water all mi life as well; that's what's kept me fit.'

Any characters you remember?

'Well ther' wer' Ben Smith, he owned the quarry and he wer' on the Council as well. I wer' t'Chairman of the Tory Club and I used to help out at election times like. I wer' Chairman of the

Summerseat Band – I couldn't play a jew's harp – but I wer' still chairman.

This is a picture of Starling Street, belonging the Ocean firm and I'd listen to complaints etc. from the workers about the houses.'

Were there any tripe works in Ramsbottom?

'No, they was in Bury. These houses here [he showed me a picture] wer' where the Heritage Society is now. It's packed out with traffic now though in Ramsbottom. I used to attend church at St. Joseph's here, but I can't get there now.

During the Second World War, they expected the use of gas warfare, so the government put black powder down all over the place in 1 cwt. drums, to combat this. After the war, the Ocean Company bought the unused drums and we re-packed the good ones and sold them abroad.

The winters wer' bad in the 1940s though, and when people wer' walking to church in clogs, they used to hide them in the hawthorn hedges and change into boots fer church, then collect the clogs after church.'

[Jim had a great collection of cuttings and photographs which he showed me, and the Ramsbottom Heritage Society have a lot of them as well.]

'I once fell thirty feet off a scaffolding at the Ocean Chemical Company. The workers took me to hospital on a corrugated sheet – there wer' no proper stretchers then. I've always kept well, but this last twelve months, I haven't been as good, but on the whole – I feel fine – fine.'

Poor Jim – only weeks after I'd spoken to him, he died quite suddenly! I'm glad I had the privilege of speaking to such a grand old man!

Black Puddings 'n' Tripe

I knocked hard at the door of the old-fashioned white-windowed shop premises on Burnley Road East, Waterfoot. For those of you who don't know, Waterfoot is at the heart of the intriguing Rossendale Valley. I say intriguing, because you never know what you're going to find next as you drive round it.

There was no answer to my knocking, and I could hear a machine inside, so I cautiously opened the door and shouted: 'Hello'. The clanking of the machine stopped momentarily, and a voice shouted back: 'Come in whoever you are – unless you're a robber'. The smell of fat and barley and blood filled my nostrils as a walked through the first room into the one behind. I wasn't quite prepared for the sight that met my eyes, though. A pretty, diminutive girl who looked about nineteen, but actually turned out to be thirty, was up to her armpits in a huge vat of what looked to be dark red mud with lumps in!

'Mary Chadwick?' I asked. 'Yes,' she replied. 'You can speak to me now, but I can't leave the work – there's only me to get the orders done.' (She was expecting me to call, as I'd 'phoned earlier, but I hadn't expected a sight like that.) Her slight figure was leaning over the vat. 'What's in there?' I asked. 'This is the filling for the puddings,' she said. 'I hope you're not squeamish, as there's all kinds of stuff in here,' she added. Well, basically I am squeamish, but I held my breath and concentrated on the questions and her replies.

I'd heard for years of the famous Chadwicks' Bury Black Puddings, but I'd never realised it was just one lady doing all the jobs. 'How did you come to be a black pudding maker?' I asked her. Mary continued to mix the filling with her hands. 'Well, it was my father's business. He took it over from Thompson's of Bury. I was an only child and at six years old I was down here turning the handle of the filling machine here.' She pointed to a contraption where the filling was poured in at the top, and then a long tube (actually a cow's intestine) was put on a special nozzle. When the handle was turned, the filling went into the intestine, and ended up as a long black sausage. 'When I left school,' said Mary, 'it was taken for granted that I went into the business with my father, who was called Edwin. That was fifteen years ago nearly, and I'm still here yet.'

Chadwicks have been famous for their delicious black puddings for years, and Mary is proud to be carrying on the tradition. I asked her what made her black puddings so popular. 'Oh well, we have our own special recipe. Basically, I use dried blood with barley and onions and some pork fat, but it's the filling that makes the pudding, so I'm not telling you what else I put in or they'll all be using it.'

Whatever it was she used certainly smelt good anyway! After Mary had used all the filling, the long black sausages were tied up into the familiar black pudding shape. Mary was tying these whilst speaking to me, and she did it so deftly and quickly that there were dozens of bunches of puddings ready in no time at all.

'I used to have two people helping me, but now I'm on my own and I find it better. I make the puddings I need for two days, then I've a stall on Bury Market for three days. I find I can do it better on my own and go at my own speed. I get lots of orders, and people come from as far away as parts of Yorkshire for my puddings. I start early in a morning – I don't have a 'brew' until dinner, then I only have a half-hour and start again, with no afternoon break.' My estimation of this enterprising young woman went up more and more as I watched how quickly and simply she did everything. No fuss – just plain, hard work!

'How many puddings do you make in a day?' I asked. 'About a thousand to fifteen hundred when I'm here,' she said. 'Have you any regular customers?' I asked. 'Oh yes – lots, a lot of people come at the same time each week. I don't know their names – just their faces.' Mary washed the tied strings of puddings under the tap. 'These are ready for boiling,' she said. Behind her were two huge boilers all ready to receive the puddings. 'I boil them for about half an hour,' she said. There were some out on a steel rack cooling from the boiler – they smelt delicious. 'Sometimes I get orders for small black puddings for dinners, and I also supply a lot of shops and retailers.' Mary put the puddings in the boiler and I watched, fascinated, as she chopped lovely pork fat for the next mix-up and filling.

'Do you sell as many in summer?' I asked. 'Almost,' said Mary. 'With all the cold summers we've had, people still want them for warmth. Old people are my main customers – the young people

Mary Chadwick putting an intestine tube on to the nozzle of the filling machine. The intestine forms the skin which holds the black pudding mixture together, and the puddings are then strung together for boiling.

won't eat them. I have people come to the stall at Bury at exactly the same time each week – you can set your watch by them.' 'It's hard work for a young woman like you, though, isn't it?' I said. Mary smiled philosophically. 'I'm used to it. I work for miself, by miself and that suits me fine. I can get on and know that it's me what'll benefit.' Brave words for one so slight and young, but Mary appeared as cheerful as anyone – in fact, even more cheerful! 'A lot of people ask for puddings to take on their holidays with them for relatives. That's why I sell a lot in summer as well,' she added. Certainly Chadwicks' black puddings are very well known in North East Lancashire, anyway.

'Before you go home you'll have to clean everything, won't you?' I asked. 'Oh yes, I swill everything first, then go all over with soda and hot soapy water. That's the hardest part when you're tired at the end of a day,' Mary told me. 'Do you live locally?' I asked. 'No,' she replied, 'I live in Mellor. I want a change of scenery when I've been here all day.'

I stood and watched Mary preparing the last batch of her famous puddings, and my admiration grew and grew. A very unusual and a very hard job for any woman, and for one so slight – even more so. But Mary is not deterred by the work which most women would find squeamish and

too heavy. She's a very enterprising young woman; cheerful, hard-working and also philosophical about the whole thing. 'It's my living, and it's up to me to make a go of it,' she said. Let's hope that she and her famous black puddings will still be around in many years to come.

As I was leaving, Mary gave me a sample of her product to take home for my family, and when my husband had eaten two black puddings, he pronounced them delicious.

––––––––––––––––––––

Following on from black puddings, of course, another very well known favourite Lancashire food was tripe, and I was lucky enough to find another lady who had inherited a business from her father – Mrs. Mary Marlow – but her father had been a tripe producer and dresser.

Mary was in 'the tripe business' from being six years old. Her father was Thomas Lord, and the business went under his name even after he'd died in 1953 and left his only child Mary to carry on. Mary worked at the business full time after she left school at fourteen, and she knows quite a lot about tripe of all kinds. When I spoke to her at her home in Rawtenstall, she was still very enthusiastic about this traditional food, and told me some interesting facts.

Tripe has a long history, being mentioned by Shakespeare in *The Taming of the Shrew*, and also by Charles Dickens in *Barnaby Rudge*. A 'Tripe Wife' was a female tripe dresser – so perhaps Mary could be regarded as one also. As the cotton trade grew in importance and work increased in Lancashire, tripe became very popular with the mill hands, because it was cheap, nourishing and easy to cook. Mary learned the art of tripe dressing from her father, serving an apprenticeship under him. Her grandfather had been a tripe dresser as well, and had been a manager at one of the famous U.C.P. (United Cattle Products) branches.

Mary remembers the branch at Bury very well, and spoke enthusiastically of how she ate there as a child. She added that tripe was much liked in Lancashire, and as well as the U.C.P. branches there were other shops providing small dining rooms in which to eat tripe etc. Many of these shops were in places like Bolton and Bury, or Burnley, some before the U.C.P. began. However, as the cotton trade declined so did the demand for tripe, people preferring more sophisticated food. Mary added that tripe dressing was very cold in winter, but that the grease helped prevent chapped hands. When it was warm in summer, then more tripe was sold and eaten cold. In

winter, it became a hot dish cooked in milk with onions.

I was surprised how much this jolly lady could remember. She said that her father had a small tripe works at Waterfoot. This is now the setting for a beautiful rest home, Scout Rest Home, and I went to the site myself to see the magnificent view. Apparently the tripe building was near a quarry, and I actually saw huge caves facing the Rest Home, which were said to extend through the hill into Crawshawbooth at the other side of the valley. These have now been blocked up, but I was told by one of the owners, Sheila Birt, that there is still a crystal clear pool in there. I could imagine Mary Marlow's father, Thomas, standing at the door of his tripe works with his hands across his white apron, looking across to St. Anne's church at Edgeside and the River Irwell below. When Mary's father died she moved into another building.

I asked her about the processes through which tripe goes before it's ready for eating. She said, 'Tripe goes through many processes. First it is collected straight from the cow at the slaughter houses after the stomach has been emptied and washed. Then the lining is removed which covers the stomach, then there are several repeated washing processes to go through, before it is ready for cooking. The protective skin covering the fat is then removed and the tripe is ready to eat. There are quite a few different parts of the tripe; honeycomb, seam, elder and dark tripe. We also produced cowheels, sheep's trotters, pigs' trotters and elder, which were all very popular dishes. Tripe and chips was a favourite in the winter. Elder is actually the udder of the cow.'

Mary continued telling me about her unusual career in tripe. 'We had stalls on Bacup and Rawtenstall markets and we were very well known all over the Rossendale Valley. Seam tripe was the most popular because it was very good,

cheap and nourishing, but all that has changed with dieting because seam is fatty. People nowadays only want the more lean, white tripe.

During the war, people used to queue for tripe to help out with the rations. Modern housewives don't want to know about tripe dishes, so the trade has declined a bit, but there are still small factories at Blackburn and Padiham producing it. Incidentally, cowheel and shin beef make a lovely potted meat. Our little stalls always did well though. I can remember the fire on Rawtenstall market in February 1948. It started in one shop, and the market hall was burned down in twenty minutes. Many traders had no insurance and lost all their stock. The following week, we opened our tripe stall, and there was only the fish stall with us. People even bought tripe to send to Scotland – they couldn't get it there. They had to use white wooden boxes, as there were no plastic ones. We always did good business – we had queues a mile long at our stall. We also sold trotters, cowheels and black puddings.'

The interview with Mary was fascinating – she told me so much in such a short time. The original tripe stall still stands on Rawtenstall market and the sign proudly states: 'Thomas Lord and Sons Tripe Dressers and Cooked Meats'. Mary's son Christopher is a teacher, and he also runs a very polished dance school in the area. He had no designs to follow in Mary's footsteps. Somebody had, however, and the ancient occupation still carries on in markets up and down our Lancashire towns.

It was unusual to meet two Marys with so much in common – both taking over from their fathers in unusual trades (for a woman, that is). The Rossendale Valley should be proud to have two such talented ladies as inhabitants.

Dialect words and phrases

in local usage

Stor thi stumps	Stir yourself. Look lively.
Mowfin.	Muffin.
Lob lolly.	Labourer.
Lob lollyin.	Doing odd jobs.
Shalla pate.	Shallow brains. Empty head.
Teed a knot wi' his tongue, he cornd undo wi' his teeth.	Put himself in a tight corner. A very difficult position.
Bitten off mooar than he can chow.	Taken too much on. Too many tasks.
Too monny irons in t'fire.	Too busy. Over zealous.
Ged agate.	Begin. Start. Commence.
Layo'ers to catch meddlars.	A trap for inquisitive people.
Galluses.	Braces.
Learned up t'top.	Full of learning. Knowledge.
T'hen hoyle.	Fowl house. Women's meeting place.
Shive o' bread.	Slice of bread.
Buttie.	Slice of bread.
Butty.	Mate, comrade. (Miners' common word.)
Ther's mooast thrutchin wheer ther's leeast room.	Uneasy crowd. Fidgeting in a crowd.
Keep a brokkun fence an loyse a naybur.	An unrepaired fence causes trouble with a neighbour. (Farmers' saying.)
Hoo's o' gam an gumption.	She's courageous and sensible.
As wick as a snig.	As lively as an eel.
Powfagged to t'deeath.	Harassed past everything.
Worried to deeath.	Worried greatly.
A'll gie thee bell-tinker.	I'll give you a hiding. (Probably connected with 'tinker' to frighten children.)
Gradely jonnock.	Said of someone who is a grand character. Honest and conscientious.

The Friends' Meeting House (left) and St. John's Church (right), Crawshawbooth.

The Weavers' Cottage
Fall Barn Fold, Rawtenstall

The long rows of windows in the weavers' cottage admitted plenty of daylight into loom-shops.

In the mid-1700s, the Rossendale Valley was fast developing as a textile producing area. At this time, it was mainly woollens, or a combination of wool and linen, that made up the bulk of the trade. Spinning and weaving were both done by handworkers until the second half of the century. Thereafter, Hargraves' Spinning Jenny, Crompton's Mule and, above all, Arkwright's Water Frame began to take over the spinning process. The vast increase in spun wool gave the weavers more to work with – but mechanised looms were much slower in developing.

Hand-loom weavers began to employ extra help: soon, they needed extra work space.

Throughout East Lancashire, efforts to provide that space were made and are still in evidence. Many farms and cottages gained extensions, marked by a row of, usually, three windows to one side of the door. Some older houses, mainly in villages or towns, simply grew another storey to create a workshop. More ambitiously, some houses, or even whole groups of houses, were purpose-built to accommodate large numbers of looms; to the extent that the living

quarters became secondary and the 'loom-shop' – forerunner of the factory – came into being.

Its life was limited. By 1800 power looms were being introduced, driven by steam, and this obviously could not be accommodated within a domestic system. The 'dark satanic mills' were about to emerge.

To say that so many weavers' premises were built, roughly over a period from 1760 to 1820 (later in Yorkshire), very few remain. This is mostly because, when their working life was done, the premises were taken over by the influx of

The 'taking-in' door can be seen at the head of the modern fire escape.

population from rural districts coming to work in the mills. Never having been intended for living in the first place, they provided very poor facilities. The woollen weavers' rooms, being in upper storeys to keep the wool dry, were far better than the 'cellar dwellings' which evolved from the damp basements created for easier working of cotton. Many of these buildings were hastily erected and became untenable quite early on; others survived until the 'Housing of the Working Classes' became a major government concern in the early years of this century. Even after that, due to two World Wars and the 1930s depression, a large number escaped demolition until the 1957 Housing Act launched a determined effort to clear slums.

Rawtenstall's weavers' cottage is a superb example of the development of both industry and housing. It is largely an earlier building enlarged and re-fronted to provide two storeys of loom space. The exact building date is unknown – research continues – but it is believed to be around the 1780–1790 period. By the 1820s Richard Ashworth, 'baize manufacturer', is listed by Baines' Directory as working at Fall Barn Fold. By 1826 the Whitehead

Brothers had introduced steam powered cotton manufacture to Rawtenstall, and the days of the handloom were numbered. However, the Whiteheads did keep several local handloom weavers on their pay roll to produce special or technically difficult pieces. The cottage at Fall Barn Fold was therefore likely to have had a longer working life than would otherwise have been expected.

The two top storeys were divided by partitions in 1890, and a new door made from a window on the ground floor to make two separate dwellings. The back half of the building, which had provided storage and service facilities, was also divided into two but the resulting accommodation was very poor. Later, in the 1920s, the front part was opened up again making quite a large and sunny house. Occupants of this part have been traced, and they all remember it as a very happy home. The back part, though, continued to deteriorate and, by 1948, conditions there left much to be desired. The premises were rented by Margaret Allen who, after a reputed argument about the rent, killed her landlady, Mrs. Chadwick. What seems to have been a particularly prosaic event has since attracted much

undue publicity and folk-legend has embroidered on it to the extent that it unfortunately overshadows the real importance of the cottage's historical presence in the town.

It also led to the abandonment and ultimate end of this part of the building. Although listed as being of historical and architectural importance in 1970, the slum clearance programme came into effect and it was demolished. It is amazing now how many people claim to have stayed the hand of the local authority from demolition of the attractive loom-shop front. Yet it was left to the newly-formed Rawtenstall Civic Society to purchase the property in February 1975 and begin a long, slow process of structural repair to bring the building back into use as a Heritage Centre for the town.

The weavers' cottage today retains much of its originality, but some compromises have had to be made to allow access for the general public. The 'takin' in door' by which bales of spun wool reached the top floor, provided a ready-made fire exit, but the earlier interior wooden staircase had to be replaced by a stone one, rescued from a demolished building in Bacup. The top floor is again opened up to its full height and length and contains a working spinning wheel and handloom, its original fireplace and much of the original ceiling. The middle floor is the Society's administration area with a small office, kitchen and meeting room, which doubles as a tea-room in summer. Downstairs are the Victorian kitchen and 'clog-shop', a small book shop and . . . well, the only way to see what happens to the cottage next is to come and see for yourselves. Having got so far, the Society's ambition is to rebuild the back part for more display space and expanding activities. The history of the weavers' cottage continues.

Kathy Fishwick
Rawtenstall Civic Society

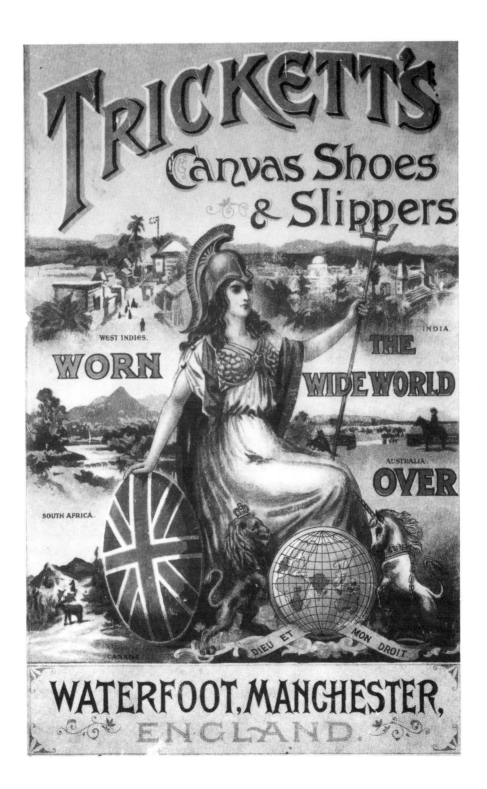